Classic Cakes and Other Great Cuisinart® Desserts

D1530475

CLASSIC CAKES

and

OTHER GREAT CUISINART® DESSERTS

Carl G. Sontheimer and Cecily Brownstone

Hearst Books / New York

Copyright © 1994 by CHC of Connecticut, Inc.

"Cuisinart" and "Cuisinarts" are registered trademarks owned by Cuisinarts Corporation.

All rights reserved. No part of this book may be reproduced or utilized in any form or by any means, electronic or mechanical, including photocopying, recording, or by any information storage or retrieval system, without permission in writing from the Publisher. Inquiries should be addressed to Permissions Department, William Morrow and Company, Inc., 1350 Avenue of the Americas, New York, N.Y. 10019.

It is the policy of William Morrow and Company, Inc., and its imprints and affiliates, recognizing the importance of preserving what has been written, to print the books we publish on acid-free paper, and we exert our best efforts to that end.

Library of Congress Cataloging-in-Publication Data

Sontheimer, Carl G.
    Classic cakes and other great Cuisinart® desserts / by Carl G. Sontheimer and Cecily Brownstone.
        p.   cm.
    Includes index.
    ISBN 0-688-12719-3
    1. Desserts.   2. Cake.   3. Food processor cookery.
I. Brownstone, Cecily.   II. Title.
TX773.S66   1994
641.8'6—dc20   93-28637
                                                           CIP

Printed in the United
States of America

First Edition

1   2   3   4   5   6   7   8   9   10

BOOK DESIGN BY RICHARD ORIOLO

ACKNOWLEDGMENTS

Among the people whose work has infused this book are Sue Jones, our food editor for so many years, and Abby Mandel, whose many creative contributions to our pages enhanced the food processor repertory. Members of our staff, among them Sue Smith, Pamela Murtagh, Barbara Conwell, Susan Weiler, Lyn Stallworth, Susan Dumont-Bengston, and Marjolein Mooney, helped shape our innovative culinary persona. Christine Goulet, our art director, gave the magazine its attractive format and, along with Jeffrey Weir of Jeffrey Weir Studios, developed its distinctive style of photography.

So many other minds and hands have contributed to this book that thanking them all here would take pages. Among the many former Cuisinart® Consumer Advisors to whom we are indebted for their help in choosing recipes are Julie Andersen, Gloria Martin, Barbara Miller, Peggy Moore, Irene Muzio, Toula Patsalis, Patsy Webb, and Diane Welsh. We also wish to thank the readers who shared their favorite recipes with us: Neils Agather, Eve Bippart, Dan Curd, Barbara Gibson, Jane Green, Nanci Jenkins, Betty Kastriner, and Sue Zwick.

Finally this page would be very lacking without special thanks to Kim Morrison and Gerrie Moore. To Gerrie, for her exceptional cooking skills and food processor know-how and her many useful suggestions during the months of testing. And to Kim, equally gifted as cook and as administrator, who created and tested in the kitchen, and organized and edited in the office, bringing her many talents to bear on getting the job done.

CONTENTS

PREFACE
"YET ONE MORE"
᷈᷈᷈

"Cookery book, of course. The truth is, there cannot be too many. Apart from usefulness, they have a charm of their own."

That is how, about sixty-five years ago, the great French chef, author, and London restaurateur X. Marcel Boulestin began his introduction to a cookbook written by his partner.

And that is how I think it is appropriate for me to begin this preface to this cookbook. Although my name is listed as co-author, it is my friend Carl Sontheimer's book.

Carl is able to offer the usefulness and charm of outstanding innovation because his passion for culinary investigation spurred him to found the food processor industry. And because, of equal importance, he has been a passionate cook and inveterate cookbook collector all his life. I have worked with him to produce this book in the hope that it will have a wide influence in breaking some century-old baking traditions, now obsolete, and replacing them with speedier and easier ways.

How do I happen to be part of this undertaking? Because my friend James Beard, who wrote in a newspaper column that "he couldn't live without a food processor," proselytized me into buying a Cuisinart® machine and introduced me to Carl. That was the beginning of Carl's and my association.

When Carl wanted to publish his magazine, *Cooking,* in a more professional way, he came to see me on a special mission. Would I be interested in using my magazine and newspaper experience to help him? Would I act as his consultant?

I accepted on one condition. As I handed him a gift, a facsimile copy of George Ellwanger's 1902 *The Pleasures of the Table,* I told him I would be happy to have my name on his masthead if he would change the name of his magazine to *The Pleasures of Cooking.* He responded with both amusement and enthusiasm. And so we have worked together on occasion—as congenially as two strong-minded, food-minded people ever can—since those days.

CECILY BROWNSTONE
New York City
January 1994

INTRODUCTION

The food processor is the most underutilized appliance in the American kitchen because most home cooks use theirs almost exclusively to chop, slice, and shred. They may turn to it for an occasional pie-crust, but never to make their other favorite pastries, cakes, cookies, puddings, or frozen desserts.

The recipes in this book will show you how to make these and many other excellent desserts in your processor faster and with less work than you may think possible. That's because food processor recipes call for simpler procedures and few extra utensils. The food processor's speed is mind-boggling: preparation time is usually cut in half. Because it makes your favorite recipes so fast and so easy, you will prepare them more often, and as you prepare them more often, they become even faster and easier.

Where do our recipes come from? In 1973, when my wife, Shirley, and I introduced the Cuisinart® food processor to America, our first test kitchen was our home kitchen. I remember the thrill of the first successful trials of the machine, from cream-puff dough to chocolate mousse. The speed and ease of making all kinds of breads, pastries, cakes, cookies, and frozen desserts in the food processor still excite me. When I think of the time and effort needed to make them in traditional ways, the shortcuts seem magical.

You can understand, then, how eager Shirley and I were to start *The Pleasures of Cooking,* the Cuisinart's® magazine. Its goal was to show cooks that using the food processor would save them time and effort in making wonderfully good meals at home.

The magazine's test kitchen started with four cooking and baking stations, later expanded to eight. Before publication each recipe was tested at least three times, then submitted to a panel of six or more tasters. The testing sheet listed preparation time and cost per serving and asked one question: "If you had made this at home, would you make it again?" Recipes earning a majority of yes answers appeared in print.

Almost from the beginning many talented chefs and food writers were happy to have the magazine publish their recipes. Among others, James Beard, Jacques Pépin, Madeleine Kamman, and Lydie Marshall contributed articles. As we grew, we were able to encourage other talented but lesser-known cooks to contribute to our magazine. Among these were Barbara Tropp and Abby Mandel. And our great staff, some of whom have become established food writers in their own right, also contributed many innovative and delightful recipes.

Here is a sampler of the dessert recipes that won so much praise for *The Pleasures of Cooking*. Many are even simpler and faster to make today, thanks to important new food processor techniques we have worked out since these recipes first appeared.

For cooks who want to cut back on cholesterol and saturated fat we have included modified versions. "The Key to Our Recipes," which follows, explains these.

Carl G. Sontheimer
Greenwich, Connecticut
January 1994

THE KEY TO OUR RECIPES

~~~~

Equipment Notes

We used a food processor whose workbowl has an inside diameter of 6 inches to test our recipes. They will not work in machines with a smaller diameter workbowl. They will work in food processors with larger diameters.

We used a 700-watt oven to test recipes with microwave instructions.

Our Two-Way Recipes

In retesting the recipes for this book we were well aware that we are in the midst of a nutritional revolution. As a result each recipe except for a few has a modified version. Where we could do so without destroying its character, we have given lower cholesterol and saturated-fat modifications that are sometimes also lower in calories.

Both the original and the modified versions taste good. Which to choose? If you prize traditional ingredients, you may wish to try an original recipe. However, if you decide its less-rich ingredients best suit your needs, we believe you will be happy choosing the modified version. Then, too, you may very well want to use an original version for company and other special occasions, a modified version for family fare.

5

About Our Modifications

Here is a rundown of the changes we made in modifying our recipes.

- In some recipes where butter flavor is essential, in the modified version we substituted margarine for only part of the butter. This preserves the buttery flavor while reducing saturated fat and cholesterol.
- Omitting egg yolks in some recipes made no difference. In others, replacing some of the yolks with egg whites yielded satisfactory results.
- In some cases, surprisingly enough, water was an adequate replacement for sour cream. In our basic recipe for cheesecake part-skim ricotta proved to be a good substitute for part of the cream cheese. In some places ricotta worked well as a substitute for part of the butter called for in a recipe.

How to Read Our Recipes

A recipe's original ingredients appear in plain type; any substitute ingredients needed for the modified version of the recipe are italicized within brackets and follow immediately afterward. To make the modified recipe, use the substitute ingredients instead of the original ones, as in the ingredient list for the cake on the next page.

GOLDEN LAYER CAKE

2 cups sugar

1½ sticks unsalted butter, cut into 12 pieces [or ½ stick unsalted butter, cut into 4 pieces, and ⅓ cup part-skim ricotta]

1 cup buttermilk

1 tablespoon vanilla extract

4 large eggs [or 2 large eggs and 3 large egg whites]

2 cups cake flour

1 tablespoon baking powder

¾ teaspoon baking soda

Pinch of salt (optional)

> To make the modified version, instead of the 1½ sticks of butter, use the bracketed ½ stick butter and ⅓ cup part-skim ricotta

> To make the modified version, instead of the 4 eggs, use the bracketed 2 eggs and 3 whites

About Our Nutritional Information

After each recipe you'll find the nutritional information pertaining to the serving given. The values for the original recipe appear first. Where a modified value is significantly different, it follows the original, separated from it by a slant bar. Here is an example:

Nutritional information per 3-ounce serving:

- calories 290 / 250
- fat 9g / 4g
- saturated fat 5g / 1g
- protein 3g
- carbohydrates 50g
- sodium 50mg / 60mg
- cholesterol 50mg / 10mg

Using Our Nutritional Information

We suggest using the nutritional information as a guide. But remember that the calorie counts and other nutritional information given for a portion or serving are always approximate, because it's not possible to measure yield or serving size exactly.

Keeping Fat Calories Legal

If you are concerned about fat consumption, here's a simple way to know whether you are keeping the calories from fat in your diet to less than the recommended 30 percent of total calories: Divide your daily calorie allowance by 10, then divide that number by 3. If the grams of fat you consume amount to less than the result, you are staying within the 30 percent guideline.

Measuring Flour

In using our recipes, measure flour by the stir, scoop, and sweep method: Stir the flour, scoop it up in a dry measure, and level it off with a straight-edged knife or spatula. This method, used in our test kitchen, gives consistent results. Spooning or sifting flour into the measuring cup will end up with as much as 20 percent less than we used.

The Hows and Whys of
Dry and Liquid Measures

Liquid measures and dry measures hold the same amount. Either can be used to measure liquids or dry ingredients; the difference is a matter of convenience:

A liquid measure has a pouring spout and is easy to lift without spilling. Liquid measures are always transparent so that they can be marked for levels less than their full capacity. These features make them convenient for measuring water, milk, and other thin liquids that level out quickly in the container.

Dry measures come in sets, usually from ¼ cup to 1 cup. Each measure holds exactly the amount marked on it. They are handy for scooping up dry ingredients and sweeping off any excess. They are also useful for measuring yogurt and other thick liquids that do not level out. Dry measures are not usually transparent.

You can measure liquids in a dry measure, but it's hard to do so without spilling when you lift it or pour from it. And you can measure dry ingredients in a liquid measure, but it's hard to do so as accurately as in a dry measure. Both liquid and dry measures are calibrated in standard U.S. cups, which contain 8 fluid ounces, or 237 milliliters each.

Not All Salts Are Equal

Our test kitchen uses table salt; if you use sea salt, you can substitute it in the same amount.

But if you use kosher salt, double the amount of salt in our recipes to get the same saltiness we did. Here's why: Because kosher salt weighs only half as much, it takes two teaspoons of it to provide the same saltiness as one teaspoon of table salt or one teaspoon of sea salt.

Using Vegetable Oils

No fat outdoes butter for flavor in cakes, cookies, and many other desserts, and most of our original recipes call for it. But it is so high in cholesterol and saturated fat that many cooks use, when it is suitable to do so, a vegetable oil with high monounsaturated and low saturated fat content. Such an oil may be better for us than margarine, which contains hydrogenated fats. Where one of these vegetable oils can replace butter without loss of taste or impairment of texture, our modified recipes call for it.

Safflower and canola oils are nutritionally suitable and readily available. So are olive oils, but many have a pronounced taste inappropriate for desserts.

For a comparison of vegetable oils, see the following table.

Saturated and Monounsaturated Content of Some Vegetable Oils*

Oil	Saturated Content (percent)	Monounsaturated Content (percent)
Canola	7.1	58
Safflower	9.1	12
Corn	12.3	24
Olive	13.5	74
Avocado	11.5	71
Almond	8.2	70
Apricot kernel	6.3	60
Hazelnut	7.4	78
Walnut	9.1	23

Source: Handbook No. 8-4, U.S. Department of Agriculture
*All vegetable oils are cholesterol free.

Food Processor Know-how

Aᴄᴄᴏʀᴅɪɴɢ to the dictionaries, the word *know-how* is defined as "the knowledge and skill required to do something smoothly and correctly." We hope some of the following suggestions will add to your ability to use the food processor easily and effectively:

- To make sure the metal blade does not fall out onto your hand when you empty the workbowl, grip the metal blade from below, placing your thumb on the outside of the workbowl and your middle finger inside the metal blade. If your metal blade is not hollow, use a spatula pressed against the hub of the blade to keep it from falling out.
- For easy removal of the last little bit from the workbowl, put it back on the machine and pulse briefly once. You can then remove the blade, which has been cleaned by centrifugal force, and the remaining contents of the workbowl are easy to scrape out.
- If making a recipe causes the food processor motor to slow down or stall, remove the workbowl contents and process the recipe in 2 batches.
- The processing times shown include time for "scraping down" where necessary. These times are approximate and intended only as a rough guide.
- When using a food processor recipe it's especially important to have all the ingredients at hand on the work surface before starting to make it. The result may suffer if the contents of the workbowl have to wait between steps.
- When a recipe calls for cutting an ingredient into 1-inch pieces, no side should be longer than 1 inch.
- When a recipe calls for pouring liquid through the feed tube, pour in a steady but unhurried stream, as you would pour coffee into a cup. But to minimize spattering when pouring in a hot liquid to melt chocolate, pour much more slowly and carefully.

CLASSIC CAKES

GOLDEN LAYER CAKE
(AND THREE VARIATIONS)
Golden Lemon Layer Cake
Golden Walnut Layer Cake
Golden Bundt Cake

SPONGE CAKE WITH HOT BLUEBERRY SAUCE

LEMON SPONGE ROLL WITH LEMON APRICOT FILLING

QUICK CHOCOLATE CAKE

GLAZED FUDGE CAKE

PAIN DE GÊNES (FRENCH ALMOND CAKE)
(AND TWO VARIATIONS)
Ring-Shaped Pain de Gênes
Pain de Gênes Base for Baked Alaska

PAIN DE GÊNES AU CHOCOLAT ET AUX NOIX DE PÉCAN
(CHOCOLATE PECAN PAIN DE GÊNES)

MACADAMIA OR HAZELNUT TORTE

APPLESAUCE CAKE

NANTUCKET CARROT CAKE

WILLIAMSBURG ORANGE WINE CAKE

PINEAPPLE UPSIDE-DOWN CAKE

SOUTHERN STRAWBERRY SHORTCAKE

PRIZE CHEESECAKE
(AND THREE VARIATIONS)
Praline Cheesecake
Apricot Cheesecake
Mocha Marble Cheesecake

CHOCOLATE CHIP POUND CAKE

SCOTCH POUND CAKE

PECAN APRICOT POUND CAKE
(AND ONE VARIATION)
Pecan Pineapple Pound Cake

One of these days when you want to try a recipe for a real American cake—for a birthday party, a holiday celebration, an anniversary, or some other special occasion—we strongly recommend our Golden Layer Cake. It has the light texture Americans favor, and you can fill and frost the layers either according to our suggestion or to suit yourself. The cake, like our others, is processed minus the many fussy steps a century of cake-making rules have deemed necessary. For a list of the chores the food processor enables you to skip in making cakes by the "creamed" method, see page 15.

Even sponge cakes, sometimes considered temperamental, are most successfully made in the food processor. We think our Sponge Cake with Hot Blueberry Sauce and our Lemon Sponge Roll with its tangy Lemon Apricot Filling will indeed please you.

When chocolate cake is the order of the day, we offer three choices. Quick Chocolate Cake has a short list of ingredients, an attractive nutritional profile, a light flavor and texture, and, true to its name, takes less than a minute to process.

Glazed Fudge Cake was devised by the vastly talented teacher and cookbook author Abby Mandel and couldn't be better. Among its fans is a New England caterer, who highlights it on her desserts list.

Pain de Gênes, Chocolate Pecan Pain de Gênes, and Macadamia or Hazelnut Torte exemplify the ease with which cakes needing a plenitude of finely chopped or ground nuts can be made in the food processor. Chocolate Pecan Pain de Gênes was developed by Kim Morrison, whose inestimable help has threaded its way through this book. We think you will be delighted with her version of Pain de Gênes.

Here, too, you'll find America's favorite cakes made with fruit— from applesauce to pineapple—in timesaving versions. And of course there's Carrot Cake, which is as good as it comes and so convenient to process.

Cheesecake also has its day. There's our prize basic version, flavored with vanilla and lemon, which, although low in rich ingredients, is heavenly creamy and flavorful. Three delicious variations follow it.

To end this delectable and serviceable round, we offer four kinds of pound cake. Take your pick.

Skipping Those Traditional, Tedious, Time-Consuming Cake-Making Steps

Cakes made by the "creamed" method call for particular steps depending on whether they are prepared in an electric mixer, or by hand with a bowl and spoon. By using the food processor you can eliminate these traditional, tedious, time-consuming steps. Here's how:

- You need not sift or stir dry ingredients together. You add each one directly to the workbowl.
- You need not add liquid and dry ingredients alternately unless a processor recipe directs you to do so. You add all the liquid in one step, before the dry ingredients, with few exceptions.
- You need not, for most recipes, take butter out of the refrigerator ahead of time to soften to room temperature. You cut a whole stick into 8 equal pieces, or cut as many tablespoon-size pieces as needed and process the butter as called for in the recipe.
- You need not beat eggs before using them or add them one at a time. You add them directly to the workbowl.
- You need not, for most recipes, melt chocolate in a separate

utensil. You melt the chocolate by putting it in the workbowl, finely chopping it with the metal blade, and pouring a heated liquid from the ingredient list through the feed tube with the motor running. Then you leave the melted chocolate in the workbowl and go on with the recipe.

- You need not use a separate utensil to grind nuts. You grind the nuts with part of the sugar or sugar and flour called for. Then you leave the mixture in the workbowl and go on with the recipe.
- You need not hand-shred such vegetables as carrots and zucchini, such fruits as apples and pears or fresh coconut. You use the fine, medium, or coarse shredding disks of the food processor.
- You need not hand-grate lemon, lime, or orange zest—the thin, outer, colored part of the peel. You remove the zest in strips with a vegetable peeler from fruit whose peel is fresh and firm and process the strips, using the metal blade, with some of the sugar or sugar and flour called for in the recipe. Then you leave the mixture in the workbowl and go on with the recipe.

Cake Pans: A Cautionary Tale

Using the standard pan—square, rectangular, or round—recommended in a reliable cake recipe ensures that the batter will fill the pan only one-half to two-thirds full, which is the optimum amount because it allows room for the batter to rise. These square and rectangular pans are about 1½ to 2 inches deep, the rectangular pans about 2 to 3 inches.

If you want to use an alternate pan, choose one that measures about the same number of square inches and is about the same depth; the batter will come up about as high as it does in the recommended pan.

To find the number of square inches in a square or rectangular pan, multiply the length by the width.

To find the number of square inches in a round pan, multiply the diameter by itself and multiply that number by 0.8.

Suppose, however, that you want to use a pan much deeper than these standard pans—say, a springform, angel food, or bundt pan. In this case, adjustments in the recipe may have to be made. For instance, a cake to be filled and frosted in 3 layers, baked in three 8-by-1½-inch pans with a total volume of 12 cups, may not be able to be made successfully in a 12-cup bundt pan (10 inches across the top and about 4 inches deep) unless some ingredient quantities are changed. Our Golden Layer Cake with its Golden Bundt Cake variation (page 20) is an example of this.

The taste and texture
of this superb cake are
unmistakably homemade,
yet it is fabulously fast
and easy to make.

Yield: 10 servings

GOLDEN LAYER CAKE

2 cups sugar

1½ sticks unsalted butter, cut into 12 pieces [or ½ stick unsalted
    butter, cut into 4 pieces, and ⅓ cup part-skim ricotta]

1 cup buttermilk

1 tablespoon vanilla extract

4 large eggs [or 2 large eggs and 3 large egg whites]

2 cups cake flour

1 tablespoon baking powder

¾ teaspoon baking soda

Pinch of salt (optional)

Preheat the oven to 375°F. Spray three 8-inch round cake pans with nonstick spray.

With the metal blade in the workbowl, process the sugar and the 1½ sticks butter [or the ½ stick butter] until smooth, about 30 seconds. Add [the ricotta], the buttermilk, the vanilla, the eggs [or the eggs and egg whites] and process until well combined, about 15 seconds. Add the remaining ingredients and pulse until they just disappear, 3 to 6 times.

Pour into the prepared pans; bake until lightly browned and a cake tester inserted in the center comes out clean, about 35 minutes. Let cool in pans on wire racks for 5 minutes; loosen sides with a small spatula and turn out onto racks to cool completely. Fill and frost as you like or with Maple Walnut Filling and Frosting for which the recipe follows:

MAPLE WALNUT FILLING AND FROSTING

½ cup walnut pieces

3¾ cups confectioners' sugar

6 tablespoons unsalted butter [or 6 tablespoons unsalted margarine], cut into 6 pieces

Pinch of salt (optional)

¾ to 1 teaspoon maple flavoring

5 to 6 tablespoons sour cream [or 4 to 5 tablespoons skim or 1% milk]

Preheat the oven to 350°F. Spread the walnuts on a baking sheet and bake until lightly toasted, 6 to 8 minutes. Remove from the oven and let cool; turn the oven off.

With the metal blade in the workbowl, process the nuts and the sugar until the nuts are finely ground, about 20 seconds. Add the butter *[or the margarine]*, the salt, and the maple flavoring and process until combined, about 15 seconds, scraping the bowl once. Add 5 tablespoons of the sour cream *[or 4 tablespoons of the milk]* and process until smooth, about 10 seconds. Check the frosting for spreading consistency, add the remaining tablespoon of sour cream *[or milk]*, if necessary.

VARIATIONS

Golden Lemon Layer Cake

Follow the recipe for Golden Layer Cake but process the zest of 1 medium lemon with ¼ cup of the sugar until the zest is finely chopped. Proceed with the Golden Layer Cake recipe. Fill and frost as desired.

Golden Walnut Layer Cake

Toast 1 cup of walnuts as directed in the Maple Walnut Filling and Frosting recipe. Process the toasted walnuts until finely chopped,

(continued) ∿

Nutritional information per serving of cake and frosting, each about 6 ounces:

calories 625 / 540

fat 26g / 16g

saturated fat 14g / 5.0g

protein 5.9g

carbohydrates 60g

sodium 123mg

cholesterol 132mg / 53mg

about 10 seconds; reserve. Follow the recipe for Golden Layer Cake and add the reserved walnuts with the flour, the baking powder, the baking soda, and the salt. For the modified recipe, substitute ¼ cup walnut oil for the ½ stick unsalted butter. Fill and frost as desired.

Golden Bundt Cake

Follow the recipe for the Golden Layer Cake, but increase the cake flour to 2¾ cups. Bake the cake in a 12-cup bundt pan, sprayed with nonstick spray, in a preheated 325°F oven until a cake tester inserted in the center comes out clean, 50 to 60 minutes. Let cool in the pan on a wire rack for 15 minutes; loosen around the side and the tube with a small spatula and turn out onto the wire rack. Ice the cake, if you like, with Vanilla or Chocolate Frosting for which the recipes follow.

VANILLA FROSTING

3 cups confectioners' sugar

Pinch of salt (optional)

2 teaspoons vanilla extract

6 tablespoons unsalted butter [or 6 tablespoons unsalted margarine], *cut into 6 pieces*

4 to 5 tablespoons sour cream [or 3 to 4 tablespoons skim or 1% milk]

With the metal blade in the workbowl, process the sugar, the salt, the vanilla, and the butter [or the margarine] until combined, about 5 seconds. Add 4 tablespoons of the sour cream [or 3 tablespoons of the milk] and process until smooth, about 10 seconds, scraping the bowl once. Check the frosting for spreading consistency and add the remaining tablespoon of sour cream [or milk] if necessary.

CHOCOLATE FROSTING

Add ¼ cup cocoa with the sugar and follow the Vanilla Frosting recipe.

Juicy Tip

Our recipe for Sponge Cake (to serve with Hot Blueberry Sauce) calls for ½ cup orange juice. You may want to use juice from fresh oranges or from frozen orange concentrate. If you choose the latter, there is no need to prepare a whole container of the concentrate. Directions for diluting it usually call for one part of concentrate to three parts of water. For the ½ cup orange juice called for in our Sponge Cake recipe, just scoop out 2 tablespoons of the concentrate and mix it with 6 tablespoons of water. For other recipes calling for varying amounts of juice, adjust the amount of concentrate and water accordingly. The opened container of concentrate, with the cover back in place, may be refrozen until the next use.

SPONGE CAKE WITH HOT BLUEBERRY SAUCE

This moist cake with its classic sponge cake flavor is delicious with either the Hot Blueberry Sauce or a bowl of fresh fruit.

Yield: 10 servings

3 strips orange zest, each 1 inch long by ½ inch wide

1 cup sugar

4 large eggs, separated [or 2 large egg yolks and 4 large egg whites]

½ cup orange juice [or ⅔ cup orange juice]

1 cup all-purpose flour

1 teaspoon baking powder [or 1½ teaspoons baking powder]

Pinch of salt (optional)

Hot Blueberry Sauce (recipe follows)

(continued)

21

Classic Cakes

*Nutritional information
per 2-ounce serving
without sauce:*

calories 200 / 180

fat 2.1g / 1.1g

saturated fat 0.6g / 0.3g

protein 3.8g

carbohydrates 40g

sodium 55mg / 45mg

cholesterol 77mg / 36mg

Yield: About 2 cups

Preheat the oven to 325°F.

With the metal blade in the workbowl, process the orange zest with the sugar until finely chopped, about 1 minute, stopping once to scrape the bowl. Add the 4 egg yolks [*or the 2 egg yolks and 2 tablespoons of the orange juice*] to the orange-sugar mixture and process for 1 minute, scraping the bowl once. With the motor running, add the orange juice [*or the remainder of the orange juice*] and process for 10 seconds. Add the flour, the baking powder, and the salt and pulse until combined, about 3 times.

In a 3-quart or larger mixing bowl, beat the egg whites with an electric mixer until stiff. With a spatula, gently but thoroughly fold the flour mixture into the beaten whites. Pour into an ungreased 10-inch tube pan with a removable bottom. Bake until the cake is lightly browned and the top springs back when gently touched, 40 to 45 minutes. Invert onto a wire rack and cool completely before removing from the pan. Serve with Hot Blueberry Sauce.

HOT BLUEBERRY SAUCE

*2 cups fresh blueberries washed and drained on paper towels,
      or 2 cups frozen blueberries*

½ cup sugar

1½ tablespoons lemon juice

¾ teaspoon grated lemon zest

½ cup water

1 teaspoon cornstarch mixed with 2 tablespoons water

In a 1½-quart saucepan bring all the ingredients except the cornstarch mixture to a boil and cook until the berries begin to burst. Add the cornstarch mixture and, stirring constantly, continue to boil just until thickened and clear, about 2 minutes.

Lemon Sponge Roll with Lemon Apricot Filling

A *light dessert with exceptionally good fruit flavor.*

~~~~~~~~~~

Yield: 12 servings

Zest of 1 lemon

¾ cup cake flour

¾ cup plus 1 tablespoon granulated sugar

3 large eggs, separated [or 1 large egg yolk and 3 large egg whites]

2 tablespoons [or ¼ cup] *lemon juice*

1 ½ teaspoons baking powder

Pinch of salt (optional)

¼ teaspoon cream of tartar

Confectioners' sugar

Lemon Apricot Filling (recipe follows)

Garnish: Whipped cream, slightly sweetened (optional)

Preheat the oven to 325°F. Line a 16-by-12-inch jelly roll pan with waxed paper, extending the paper 2 inches beyond the ends of the pan. Spray the paper with nonstick spray.

With the metal blade in the workbowl, process the zest with ¼ cup of the flour and ¼ cup of the granulated sugar until the zest is finely chopped, about 1 minute. Add ½ cup more of the granulated sugar, the 3 yolks [or the 1 yolk] and the lemon juice and process until thick and light colored, 30 to 40 seconds. Add the remaining flour, the

(continued) ~

*Nutritional information
per 2½-ounce serving:*

  calories 190

  fat 4.9g

  saturated fat 2.3g

  protein 2.6g

  carbohydrates 38g

  sodium 23mg

  cholesterol 103mg / 71mg

baking powder and the salt; pulse until flour disappears, 3 to 4 times. Transfer the mixture to a large mixing bowl.

In another mixing bowl, beat the egg whites and the cream of tartar with an electric mixer until soft peaks form; add the remaining 1 tablespoon sugar and continue beating until the whites are stiff but not dry. Fold one quarter of the beaten egg whites into the yolk mixture, then fold in the remaining whites gently but thoroughly.

Spread the batter evenly in the prepared pan. Bake until barely golden or a cake tester inserted in the center comes out clean, 15 to 18 minutes. Sift about 1 tablespoon confectioners' sugar over the cake, cover it with waxed paper and a damp towel, and invert it. Let the cake cool for 5 minutes, peel off the top sheet of paper, and invert onto another towel that has been sprinkled with confectioners' sugar. Remove the remaining paper from the cake and spread it with the Lemon Apricot Filling. Roll it up, using the towel to lift it. Refrigerate until serving time. Sprinkle with confectioners' sugar before serving. Pass the whipped cream if you like.

LEMON APRICOT FILLING

8 dried apricots

1 cup sugar

1 tablespoon cornstarch

Pinch of salt (optional)

¼ cup lemon juice

3 tablespoons unsalted butter, melted

1 large egg

2 large egg yolks

In a 1-quart saucepan, poach the apricots in ½ cup water until they are soft, about 15 minutes; drain.

With the metal blade in the workbowl, process the apricots until they are finely chopped, about 20 seconds. Add the sugar, the cornstarch, and the salt and process until smooth, about 30 seconds. Add the lemon juice, the melted butter, the egg, and the egg yolks and process until thick and smooth, about 15 seconds.

Transfer the mixture to a 1-quart saucepan and cook over medium-low heat, stirring constantly until thick, about 12 minutes. Do not let the mixture come to a boil. Put the mixture in a small bowl, cover tightly, and refrigerate for at least 1 hour before using. Use as directed.

This cake combines delicate chocolate flavor with a light, airy texture.

~~~~~~~~~

Yield: 10 servings

QUICK CHOCOLATE CAKE

~~~

1 large egg
2 large egg whites
1 cup sugar
1/2 cup cocoa
2/3 cup vegetable oil [or 2 tablespoons vegetable oil and 3 tablespoons part-skim ricotta]
1/2 cup milk [or 1/2 cup skim or 1% milk]
1 teaspoon vanilla extract
2/3 cup all-purpose flour
2 teaspoons baking powder
Chocolate Icing (recipe follows)

Preheat the oven to 350°F. Spray a 9-inch round cake pan with non-stick spray.

With the metal blade in the workbowl, process the egg, the egg whites, and the sugar until foamy, about 20 seconds. Add the cocoa, the oil [or the oil and ricotta], the milk, and the vanilla. Process until well combined, about 20 seconds. Add the flour and the baking powder; pulse until the flour disappears, about 5 times, scraping the bowl as needed. Pour into the prepared pan and bake until a cake tester inserted in the center comes out clean, 25 to 30 minutes.

Let cool in pan on a wire rack for 10 minutes; loosen edge with a small spatula and turn out onto rack to finish cooling.

CHOCOLATE ICING

7 ounces semisweet chocolate

¼ cup water

*5 tablespoons unsalted margarine, cut into 5 equal pieces and
allowed to soften*

Place the chocolate and the water in a small saucepan. Melt over low
heat. Stir in the margarine, piece by piece; the resulting icing should
be smooth, shiny, and quite liquid. Place a wire rack with the cake
on it over a sheet of waxed paper under the rack. Pour icing slowly
onto top and let it dribble down the side. It will firm up on standing.

*Nutritional information
per serving of cake, each
about 2⅓ ounces:*

    calories 265 / 168

    fat 15g / 4.2g

    saturated fat 1.2g / 0.7g

    protein 3.6g / 4.1g

    carbohydrates 31g

    sodium 92mg

    cholesterol 22mg

*Nutritional information
per serving of cake and
icing, each about 3⅓
ounces:*

    calories 408 / 311

    fat 28g / 16g

    saturated fat 2.3g / 1.7g

    protein 5.0g

    carbohydrates 43g

    sodium 93mg

    cholesterol 22mg

GLAZED FUDGE CAKE

~~~

This is a true chocolate lover's cake: dark, moist, and so rich-tasting, it can be served without a frosting.

~~~~~~~~

Yield: 12 servings

2 squares (1 ounce each) unsweetened baking chocolate, broken into pieces

1¼ cups sugar

⅓ cup boiling water

1 tablespoon cocoa [or omit]

2 large eggs [or 1 large egg and 2 large egg whites]

1½ sticks unsalted butter, cut into 12 pieces [or ⅓ cup part-skim ricotta and 2 tablespoons vegetable oil]

½ cup sour cream [or ½ cup buttermilk]

1 tablespoon dark rum [or 1 teaspoon vanilla extract]

½ teaspoon salt (optional)

¾ cup plus 2 tablespoons cake flour [or 1 cup cake flour]

1 teaspoon baking powder

½ teaspoon baking soda

Chocolate Rum Glaze (recipe follows)

Preheat the oven to 325°F. Spray an 8-inch springform pan with non-stick spray.

With the metal blade in the workbowl, process the chocolate and ¼ cup of the sugar until chocolate is finely chopped, about 1 minute. With the motor running, pour the hot water slowly through the feed tube and process until chocolate is melted, about 20 seconds.

Add the remaining sugar, the cocoa, the eggs [or the egg and egg whites], the butter [or the ricotta and oil], the sour cream [or the buttermilk], the rum [or the vanilla] and the salt; process for 1 minute, scraping the bowl once. Add the remaining ingredients and pulse until the flour just disappears, about 3 times.

Pour into the prepared pan. Bake until a cake tester inserted in the center comes out clean, 50 to 60 minutes, then turn out onto a wire rack to finish cooling. Prepare the Chocolate Rum Glaze. When the cake is cool, spread the glaze over the top and sides with a spatula.

CHOCOLATE RUM GLAZE

3 ounces German sweet chocolate, broken into 6 pieces

2 tablespoons water

2 tablespoons unsalted butter [or 2 tablespoons unsalted margarine]

4 tablespoons confectioners' sugar

1 teaspoon dark rum [or 1 teaspoon vanilla extract]

Put all the ingredients, except the rum [or the vanilla], in the top of a double boiler. Cook slowly over hot water until the chocolate is melted, stirring gently. Add the rum [or the vanilla], stir, and refrigerate the glaze until it begins to thicken.

Nutritional information per 3-ounce serving:

calories 337 / 245

fat 21g / 10g

saturated fat 11g / 2.5g

protein 3.0g

carbohydrates 36g

sodium 81mg / 96mg

cholesterol 75mg / 20mg

Pain de Gênes is a French cake of old and classical tradition. It has a marked almond flavor. In France both sweet and bitter almonds are used to produce its unique taste. Because importing bitter almonds into this country is illegal (they contain a small amount of the deadly poison cyanide), we use sweet almonds plus almond extract to give the traditional fine flavor.

The classic French recipe for Pain de Gênes calls for separating eggs, beating their whites stiff, and folding them into the batter. With the use of the food processor, we prepare the cake using whole eggs plus a little baking powder and omit the extra step.

If almond flavor really pleases you and you like European cakes that are on the dense but moist side, we think you will truly enjoy this almond Pain de Gênes. Devotees of pecans will prefer its pecan-and-chocolate-flavored mate.

Its subtle flavor of sweet almonds and soft, moist texture have made this cake as popular in France today as it was two hundred years ago. Our American tasters also gave it high marks.

Yield: 10 servings

PAIN DE GÊNES

(FRENCH ALMOND CAKE)

½ cup minus 2 tablespoons all-purpose flour

¾ cup blanched almonds

½ teaspoon baking powder

¾ cup sugar

2 teaspoons vanilla extract

¼ teaspoon almond extract

1 stick unsalted butter, melted [or 2 tablespoons unsalted butter, melted, and ¼ cup vegetable oil]

3 large eggs [or 1 large egg and 3 large egg whites]

Spray a 9-inch round cake pan with nonstick spray.

With the metal blade in the workbowl, process the flour, the almonds, and baking powder for 2 minutes. The mixture will be almost as smooth as flour. Add the remaining ingredients and pulse until flour disappears, about 5 times, scraping the bowl as necessary. Pour the batter into the prepared pan and place in a cold oven. Set the oven temperature at 300°F; bake until a cake tester inserted in the center comes out clean, 35 to 40 minutes.

Let cool in pan on a wire rack for 10 minutes. Loosen side with a small spatula, turn out onto the rack, and let cool completely. Sprinkle with confectioners' sugar before serving.

VARIATIONS

Ring-Shaped Pain de Gênes

To bake the Pain de Gênes in a 6½-cup ring mold (9½ inches top diameter and 2 inches high), follow the directions given above for preparing the Pain de Gênes in a 9-inch round pan, but increase the baking time to 45 to 50 minutes and use the following ingredients:

½ cup all-purpose flour

1 cup blanched almonds

¾ teaspoon baking powder

1 cup sugar

1 tablespoon vanilla extract

½ teaspoon almond extract

1⅓ sticks unsalted butter, melted [or 3 tablespoons unsalted butter, melted, and ⅓ cup vegetable oil]

4 large eggs [or 2 large eggs and 3 large egg whites]

Nutritional information per 2-ounce serving:

calories 240 / 220

fat 16g / 14g

saturated fat 6.7g / 2.4g

protein 4.5g

carbohydrates 21g

sodium 40mg

cholesterol 89mg / 27mg

Yield: 16 servings

Nutritional information per 1½-ounce serving:

calories 200 / 165

fat 13g / 10g

saturated fat 5.5g / 1.9g

protein 4.3g / 3.7g

carbohydrates 18g / 16g

sodium 18mg

cholesterol 74mg / 29mg

(continued)

*Nutritional information
per ¾-ounce serving:*
calories 84 / 77
fat 5.5g / 4.8g
saturated fat 2.3g / 0.7g
protein 1.8g
carbohydrates 7.8g
sodium 7.7mg / 6.8mg
cholesterol 31mg / 12mg

Pain de Gênes Base for Baked Alaska

To bake the Pain de Gênes base for Baked Alaska in an 8-inch round pan, follow the directions given on page 31 for preparing the Pain de Gênes in a 9-inch round pan, but decrease the baking time to 25 to 30 minutes and use the following ingredients:

¼ cup all-purpose flour

½ cup blanched almonds

½ teaspoon baking powder

½ cup sugar

1½ teaspoons vanilla extract

¼ teaspoon almond extract

⅔ stick unsalted butter, melted [or 1 tablespoon unsalted butter, melted, and 3 tablespoons vegetable oil]

2 large eggs [or 1 large egg and 1 large egg white]

Pain de Gênes au Chocolat et aux Noix de Pécan

(CHOCOLATE PECAN PAIN DE GÊNES)

~~~

1 ¼ cups pecan halves

¼ cup all-purpose flour

3 tablespoons cocoa

½ teaspoon baking powder

¾ cup sugar

1 teaspoon vanilla extract

1 stick unsalted butter, melted [or 2 tablespoons unsalted butter, melted, and 6 tablespoons part-skim ricotta]

3 large eggs [or 1 large egg and 3 large egg whites]

Preheat the oven to 350°F.

Spread the pecans on a baking sheet and bake until the nuts are lightly toasted, about 6 to 8 minutes. Turn the oven off.

Spray a 9-inch round cake pan with nonstick spray.

With the metal blade in the workbowl, process the flour, the pecans, the cocoa, and the baking powder until the pecans are finely chopped, about 30 seconds. The mixture will be almost as smooth as flour.

Add the remaining ingredients and pulse until they just disappear, about 5 times, scraping the bowl as necessary. Pour the batter into the prepared pan and place in a cold oven. Set the oven temperature

(continued) ~

The combination of chocolate and pecans in this unusual version of a French specialty is so outstanding that this cake needs no frosting or other embellishment.

~~~~~~~~

Yield: 12 servings

Nutritional information per 1¾-ounce serving:

  calories 270 / 210

  fat 20g / 13g

  saturated fat 7.6g / 2.8g

  protein 3.7g

  carbohydrates 21g

  sodium 40mg / 50mg

  cholesterol 89mg / 30mg

at 300°F; bake until a cake tester inserted in the center comes out clean, 40 to 45 minutes.

Let cool on a wire rack for 10 minutes. Loosen side with a small spatula. Turn out onto a rack and let cool completely. Sprinkle with confectioners' sugar before serving.

Toasting Hazelnuts: A Must

To achieve the wonderful intensity of flavor hazelnuts offer, they must be toasted and have their skins removed. Here is a method we find eminently successful for doing just that. Wherever we call for toasted hazelnuts in this book, you'll find a reference to this page.

Preheat the oven to 350°F. Spread the amount of hazelnuts you need on an ungreased baking sheet and bake until lightly toasted, 8 to 10 minutes. To test, break one open to see if it looks light brown inside. Do not overbake. While the nuts are still very warm, rub them vigorously in a towel to remove as much of the skin as you can.

Macadamia or Hazelnut Torte

～～～

7 ounces (about 1½ cups) macadamia nuts or hazelnuts

½ cup all-purpose flour

1 teaspoon baking powder

1 cup sugar

6 large eggs, separated [or 2 large eggs and 6 large egg whites]

1 teaspoon vanilla extract

Caramel Sauce (recipe follows)

Place oven rack just below center of oven. Preheat the oven to 350°F. Spray a 10-by-4-inch angel food pan with nonstick spray.

Brush the salt off the macadamias if you like; or, if using, toast the hazelnuts according to the directions on page 34.

With the metal blade in the workbowl, process the flour, the baking powder, ½ cup of the sugar, and the nuts until the nuts are finely chopped, about 60 seconds, scraping the bowl once. Reserve.

Process the remaining ½ cup sugar, the 6 egg yolks [or the 2 whole eggs], and the vanilla until thick and pale yellow, about 40 seconds, scraping the bowl as necessary.

In a large mixing bowl, beat the egg whites with an electric mixer until stiff. With a spatula, fold the egg mixture into the beaten whites. Sprinkle the reserved nut mixture on top and fold in gently but thoroughly.

Pour the batter into the prepared pan and bake until a cake tester comes out clean, 30 to 35 minutes. Let the cake cool completely in the pan on a wire rack. Run a small spatula around the edge and invert onto a serving plate. Serve with Caramel Sauce.

(continued) ～

These are delicate, light-textured cakes. If you prefer a subtle flavor, choose the macadamia version; the hazelnut variation is more intense. The Caramel Sauce enhances both without overpowering them.

～～～～～～

Yield: 6 servings

Nutritional information per 1½-ounce serving

calories 160 / 150

fat 10g / 9g

saturated fat 1.7g

protein 3.3g

carbohydrates 16g

sodium 23mg

cholesterol 72mg / 24g

Caramelizing Sugar

Caramelized sugar gives a delicious taste to recipes like our Caramel Sauce. It is made by cooking sugar until it melts and turns golden or light brown in color. Some cooks consider it difficult, but we hope the following suggestions will be helpful:

Stir the sugar and water together, but you need not stir after the sugar dissolves.

Watch attentively for the first hint of color change from crystal clear to faintly golden. If the melted sugar colors evenly, don't stir, but if it colors unevenly, stir only with a wooden spoon. A metal spoon will cool the melted sugar, causing it to crystallize immediately on the spoon.

As soon as the sugar turns a rich golden color, remove the pan from the heat and follow the next step in the recipe.

Yield: 1 cup

Nutritional information per tablespoon:
calories 50
fat 0.9g
saturated fat 0.5g
protein 0.1g
carbohydrates 11g
sodium 1.9mg
cholesterol 3.0mg

36

C l a s s i c

C a k e s

CARAMEL SAUCE

3 tablespoons water

1 cup sugar

1/3 cup light cream, at room temperature

1 teaspoon vanilla extract

In a 1-quart saucepan over medium heat, stir together the water and the sugar until well mixed; bring to the boil over high heat. Reduce the heat to medium-high and continue cooking until the syrup just begins to turn golden brown, about 5 to 10 minutes; do not stir. Remove from the heat and carefully whisk in the light cream and vanilla in a slow steady stream; caramel will foam when light cream is added. Whisk until the sauce is smooth; if necessary to dissolve any lumps of caramelized sugar, place over very low heat and continue whisking until smooth.

APPLESAUCE CAKE

❧❧❧

20 walnut halves

½ cup walnut pieces

1½ pounds Granny Smith apples, peeled, cored, and quartered

1¾ cups all-purpose flour

1¾ cups sugar

1 teaspoon baking soda

½ teaspoon salt (optional)

½ teaspoon ground nutmeg

1 teaspoon ground cinnamon

¼ teaspoon ground cloves

3 large eggs [or 1 large egg and 3 large egg whites]

1 stick unsalted butter, cut into 8 pieces [or 2 tablespoons vegetable oil and ⅓ cup part-skim ricotta]

1 cup raisins

Vanilla Frosting (recipe follows)

Preheat the oven to 350°F. Spread the walnuts on a baking sheet, keeping the halves apart from the pieces, and bake until well browned, 6 to 8 minutes. Remove from the oven and reserve.

In a 1½-quart or larger microwave-safe bowl, microwave the apples uncovered on full power until reduced in volume to between 1⅓ and 1½ cups. This will take about 15 to 20 minutes in a 700-watt oven; stir twice during cooking. Let cool and reserve. (Or cook apples in a steamer on top of the range.)

Spray a 13-by-9-by-2-inch baking pan with nonstick spray.

(continued) ❧

A classic cake that originated in the United States is brought up-to-date: The apples for it may be cooked in minutes in the microwave and the batter is mixed in seconds in the food processor. But it still tastes so heartwarmingly good that Americans in every part of our country still favor it.

❧❧❧❧❧❧❧

Yield: 20 servings

*Nutritional information
per 3-ounce serving:*

calories 290 / 247

fat 9.3g / 4.4g

saturated fat 4.6g / 0.9g

protein 2.9g / 3.4g

carbohydrates 51g

sodium 53mg / 61mg

cholesterol 50mg / 13mg

To the workbowl with the metal blade, add the flour, the sugar, the baking soda, the salt, the nutmeg, the cinnamon, the cloves, the eggs *[or the egg and egg whites]*, the butter *[or the oil and ricotta]*, and the reserved apples. Process until well mixed, about 20 seconds. Add the raisins and the walnut pieces. Pulse only until the raisins and walnuts disappear below the surface, about 3 times; do not overprocess.

Turn into the prepared pan and bake until a cake tester inserted in the center comes out clean, about 40 minutes. Cool cake in pan on a wire rack. When the cake has cooled to room temperature, spread the Vanilla Frosting over the top. Garnish with the reserved walnut halves.

VANILLA FROSTING

2 cups confectioners' sugar

*½ stick unsalted butter, cut into 4 pieces [or 1 tablespoon unsalted
    butter and 3 tablespoons part-skim ricotta]*

*1 large egg white or 1 tablespoon dried egg white and 2
    tablespoons water (see page 39) [or 1 tablespoon water]*

1 teaspoon vanilla extract

With the metal blade in the workbowl, process all the ingredients to a smooth consistency, about 20 seconds. If the frosting is too thick, add cold water by the teaspoonful, processing after each addition until easily spreadable. Use as directed.

Ever Try Dried Egg Whites?

The cholesterol in an egg is all concentrated in the yolk. That's why many recipes which a few years ago called for whole eggs now substitute egg whites for part or all of these. But the white as well as the yolk of an egg may contain salmonella, and fear of salmonella poisoning causes many people to avoid recipes that use raw egg whites.

Whatever the risk of salmonella poisoning may be, powdered dried egg whites provide an easy way to eliminate it. They are salmonella-free and readily available by mail order. We have found they replace the fresh variety in mousses, meringues, and other uncooked desserts with little, if any, change in the result. Of course there is no need to use them in cakes and cookies that are fully cooked.

To replace 1 fresh egg white, use 1 tablespoon of the egg-white powder and 2 tablespoons cold water. Put the water in a container with a tight-fitting cover, sprinkle the egg-white powder over it, put on the cover, and shake vigorously. Use this mixture as you would 1 fresh egg white.

Dried egg whites are available nationally by mail order from DEB-EL Foods Corporation, P.O. Box 876, Elizabeth, NJ 07206. Other sources and information on low-cholesterol whole-egg products may be available from the American Egg Board, 1460 Renaissance Drive, Park Ridge, Illinois 60068.

Once upon a time a little harborside café on Nantucket Island was famous for its Carrot Cake, the creation of a talented young chef. She bestowed her recipe on us, and we have been happy to pass it along ever since.

∿∿∿∿∿∿

Yield: 16 servings

NANTUCKET CARROT CAKE

∿∿∿

2 medium (8 ounces total) carrots, peeled

1 cup all-purpose flour

1 teaspoon baking powder

1 teaspoon baking soda

½ teaspoon salt (optional)

1 teaspoon ground cinnamon

1 cup sugar

2 large eggs [or 3 large egg whites]

¾ cup vegetable oil [or 1 tablespoon vegetable oil and ¼ cup part-skim ricotta]

½ cup pecan halves

Cream Cheese Frosting (recipe follows)

Garnish: Extra pecan halves (optional)

Spray an 8½ by 4½ by 2½-inch (5-cup) loaf pan with nonstick spray. Preheat the oven to 325°F.

Shred the carrots with the fine shredding disk or hand-grate them fine; there should be 1½ cups shredded carrots, tightly packed; reserve.

With the metal blade in the workbowl, pulse the remaining ingredients, except the pecans, until well-mixed, about 4 times. Add the reserved carrots and pecans; pulse only until evenly distributed, about 4 times. Do not overprocess.

∿

Pour into the prepared pan and bake until a cake tester inserted in the center comes out clean, about 60 minutes. Loosen the sides with a small spatula and turn out onto a wire rack. Let cool completely. Spread Cream Cheese Frosting over the top and sides of the cake. Garnish, if you like, with extra pecan halves.

CREAM CHEESE FROSTING

½ stick unsalted butter [or ½ stick unsalted margarine], *cut into 4 pieces*

4 ounces cream cheese [or 4 ounces Neufchâtel cheese*], *cut into 4 pieces*

1 teaspoon vanilla extract

1¾ cups confectioners' sugar

With the metal blade in the workbowl, process all the ingredients until smooth.

Nutritional information per 2½-ounce serving:

calories 308 / 215

fat 19g / 7.8g

saturated fat 4.5g / 1.0g

protein 2.7g / 3.1g

carbohydrates 35g

sodium 106mg / 130mg

cholesterol 42mg / 3.6mg

*Neufchâtel is usually sold as a light cream cheese. It is a natural cheese with less fat than cream cheese.

Historical Cake

More than fifty years ago Mrs. Helen Bullock, an archivist for the restoration of Virginia's Colonial Williamsburg, uncovered a splendid recipe for Williamsburg Orange Wine Cake and published it in *The Williamsburg Art of Cookery or, Accomplish'd Gentlewoman's Companion*. Its fame spread to every section of the country. No wonder. Of its kind, the cake is as delicious as you are likely to encounter. Indeed, one version of it won a 1950 $25,000 bake-off prize. Interestingly enough, this old-time cake is particularly appropriate for the new-time food processor because it chops the orange peel, walnuts, and raisins—a great flavor combination—right into the batter.

This famous cake offers you a choice of toppings—both utterly delicious.

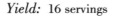

Yield: 16 servings

WILLIAMSBURG ORANGE WINE CAKE

1 medium (8 ounces) thick-skinned orange, washed and dried

1 cup sugar

1 teaspoon vanilla extract

1 cup buttermilk

2 large eggs [or 3 large egg whites]

1 stick unsalted butter, cut into 8 pieces [or 3 tablespoons vegetable oil and ¼ cup part-skim ricotta]

2 cups all-purpose flour

1 teaspoon baking soda

½ cup walnut halves

1 cup raisins

Orange Glaze or Williamsburg Wine Icing (recipes follow)

Preheat the oven to 350°F. Spray a 9-inch square pan with nonstick spray.

With a sharp knife, score the orange with 8 equally spaced vertical cuts. Slip your thumb under the peel at the top and pull off the peel in 8 sections; set aside. Only the peel is used in this recipe. If you plan to use the Williamsburg Wine Icing, set aside 1 section of peel for the icing, reserving the remaining 7 for the cake.

With the metal blade in the workbowl, process the orange peel and the sugar until the peel is finely chopped, about 60 seconds, scraping the workbowl as needed. Add the vanilla, the buttermilk, the eggs [or the egg whites], and the butter [or the oil and ricotta]. Process until well combined, about 15 seconds. Add the flour, the baking soda, the walnuts, and the raisins. Pulse until the flour just disappears, 3 to 5 times. Pour into the prepared pan and bake until a cake tester inserted in the center comes out clean, 30 to 35 minutes.

If you intend to use the Orange Glaze, prepare it while the cake is baking and spoon it evenly over the cake as soon as it comes out of the oven. Return the cake to the oven for 5 minutes. Let cool in the pan on a wire rack. Cut into 16 serving squares before removing from the pan.

To use the Williamsburg Wine Icing, let the cake cool in the pan on a wire rack for 10 minutes; loosen the sides with a small spatula and turn out onto rack. Let cool completely. Spread Williamsburg Wine Icing evenly over the top and sides.

ORANGE GLAZE

In a small bowl, stir together ½ cup sugar and 3 tablespoons orange juice. The sugar will dissolve when the mixture is poured on the hot cake and returned to the oven for 5 minutes.

Nutritional information per serving of cake, each about 2½ ounces:

calories 226 / 198

fat 8.6g / 5.3g

saturated fat 4.0g / 0.7g

protein 4.0g

carbohydrates 35g

sodium 78mg

cholesterol 42mg / 2.0mg

Nutritional information per serving of cake and glaze, each about 2¾ ounces:

calories 250 / 223

fat 8.6g / 5.3g

saturated fat 4.0g / 0.7g

protein 4.0g

carbohydrates 42g

sodium 78mg

cholesterol 42mg / 1.9mg

(continued) ∽

43

Classic

Cakes

*Nutritional information
per serving of cake and
icing, each about 3¼
ounces:*

calories 315 / 286

fat 12g / 8.4g

saturated fat 6.1g / 1.3g

protein 4.2g

carbohydrates 50g

sodium 82mg

cholesterol 52mg / 2mg

WILLIAMSBURG WINE ICING

2 cups confectioners' sugar

*Reserved section of orange peel from Williamsburg Orange Wine
    Cake recipe*

1 tablespoon dry sherry

*5 tablespoons unsalted butter [or 5 tablespoons unsalted margarine], cut
    into 5 pieces*

1 large egg white [or 1 tablespoon water]

With the metal blade in the workbowl, process the confectioners'
sugar and orange peel until the peel is finely chopped, about 60 seconds. Add the sherry, the butter [or the margarine], and the egg white
[or the water] and process until smooth, about 15 seconds. If the icing
is too thick, add up to 1 teaspoon more sherry, a few drops at a time,
until easily spreadable.

American Classic

Pineapple Upside-down Cake is one of America's famous creations, but its
inventor remains unsung. No one, to our knowledge, has discovered who
developed the recipe for it or when it was first published. By the mid-1920s,
however, we can tell that the dessert was well known because there were as
many as 2,500 entries for it in a pineapple recipe contest. Obviously it was
a favorite in a good many American families. By the time the 1930s rolled
around, recipes for it began to appear in our comprehensive cookbooks.

Over the years Pineapple Upside-down Cake has changed—for the better.
Originally the cake was made with a hefty amount of batter. Nowadays many
cooks use a slimmer cake layer; our recipe goes along with this. And another
change: In the early days the cake was often made in a black iron skillet,
whereas today a round cake pan is usually used.

Which Kind?

The flavor of light brown sugar is on the subtle side, while that of dark brown sugar is much more intense. Whenever a recipe calls for brown sugar, we specify the kind we believe benefits it most. We do not recommend granulated brown sugar.

PINEAPPLE UPSIDE-DOWN CAKE

America's cherished old-fashioned dessert now has a plus: The food processor whips up its cake portion in a matter of seconds.

Yield: 8 servings

One 20-ounce can unsweetened sliced pineapple (10 slices)

1 stick unsalted butter [or 2 tablespoons unsalted butter and 6 tablespoons unsalted margarine], *cut into 8 pieces*

½ cup firmly packed light brown sugar

1 cup all-purpose flour

2 teaspoons baking powder

¾ cup sugar

1 large egg [or 2 large egg whites]

½ cup milk [or ½ cup skim or 1% milk]

1 teaspoon vanilla extract

8 candied red cherries

1 cup heavy cream, whipped until stiff and flavored with vanilla and a suspicion of sugar (optional)

(continued)

45
Classic Cakes

*Nutritional information
per 4½-ounce serving:*

calories 290

fat 11g

saturated fat 7.0g / 3.3g

protein 3.1g

carbohydrates 46g

sodium 24mg

cholesterol 54mg / 8.8mg

Preheat the oven to 350°F.

Drain 8 slices of the pineapple; 2 slices and the juice will not be used in this recipe.

In a 9-inch round cake pan, over very low heat, stir half the butter *[or 4 tablespoons of the margarine]* until melted but still creamy. Remove the pan from the heat. Add the brown sugar and stir until combined. Spread evenly over the bottom of the pan. Arrange the 8 pineapple slices (one in the center) over the sugar mixture. Reserve.

With the metal blade in the workbowl, process the remaining ingredients until smooth, 12 to 15 pulses, scraping the bowl as necessary. Pour the batter over the pineapple and spread evenly.

Bake until a cake tester inserted in the center comes out clean, 35 to 45 minutes. Let cool on a wire rack for 5 minutes. Loosen side with a small spatula. Invert onto a serving plate. Garnish the center of each pineapple slice with a cherry. Serve warm. Pass the whipped cream if you like.

Individual Pineapple Upside-down Cakes

To make 8 individual Pineapple Upside-down Cakes, substitute 12 pineapple chunks from an 8-ounce can for the pineapple slices. Cut the pineapple chunks into quarters. Reserve.

In a small saucepan, stir half of the butter *[or 4 tablespoons of the margarine]* over low heat until melted but still creamy. Remove the pan from the heat. Add the brown sugar and stir until combined. Divide the mixture evenly among eight 6-ounce custard cups. In each cup, arrange 6 pieces of the reserved pineapple in a petal design.

Make the cake batter as directed and divide equally among the custard cups. Place the cups on a baking sheet and bake until the tops are lightly browned and a cake tester inserted in the center of one comes out clean, 20 to 25 minutes. Let cool on a wire rack for 5 minutes. Invert onto individual serving plates. Garnish the center of each cake with a cherry half. Serve warm. Pass whipped cream if you like.

Southern Secret

New Englanders are staunch believers in Strawberry Shortcake made with biscuits drenched with berries and "pour" cream. New Yorkers defend Strawberry Shortcake concocted of layers of sponge cake laced with berries and whipped cream. But some southern families keep their choice secret: They quietly favor Strawberry Shortcake that boasts rich pastry sandwiched together with berries and whipped cream, then gloriously topped with more of the same. Not well known, but so good.

SOUTHERN STRAWBERRY SHORTCAKE

If you have never tasted Strawberry Shortcake made with two layers of pastry instead of biscuit or cake, you are in for a delightful surprise.

Yield: 12 servings

¾ cup all-purpose flour

¼ teaspoon salt (optional)

6 tablespoons unsalted butter [or 2 tablespoons unsalted butter and 4 tablespoons unsalted margarine], *chilled and cut into 6 pieces*

2 tablespoons ice water

1 pint fresh strawberries, hulled

1½ cups heavy cream, whipped and sweetened to taste

(continued)

47

Classic Cakes

*Nutritional information
per 2½-ounce serving:*

calories 193

fat 17g

saturated fat 10g / 8.8g

protein 1.7g

carbohydrates 9.4g

sodium 12mg

cholesterol 56mg / 46mg

To the workbowl with the metal blade, add the flour, the salt, and the butter *[or the butter and margarine]*. Pulse until the mixture resembles coarse crumbs, 3 to 5 times. Drizzle the ice water over the mixture and pulse until the mixture just holds together, 3 to 4 times. Do not overprocess.

Remove the dough from the workbowl and divide it in half. Shape each portion into a disk, wrap in plastic wrap, and refrigerate for at least 2 hours.

On a lightly floured surface, roll out each disk into an 8-inch-diameter and ⅛-inch-thick circle. Place an 8-inch lid or cake pan on the dough and cut around it with a sharp knife to make it even; place both rounds of dough on an ungreased cookie sheet and prick at 2-inch intervals with a fork. Refrigerate for 30 minutes.

Preheat the oven to 400°F.

Bake until the edges are lightly browned, 10 to 12 minutes. With a large metal spatula, carefully transfer the pastry rounds to wire racks and let cool.

Use the medium slicing disk to slice the strawberries. Reserve a few slices for garnish and fold the rest into the whipped cream. Place one of the pastry rounds on a serving dish and cover with half of the strawberry mixture; place the other pastry layer on top and cover with the remaining strawberry mixture. Garnish with the reserved sliced strawberries.

PRIZE CHEESECAKE

❧

1 double graham cracker (5 by 2½ inches), broken into 4 pieces

1 envelope unflavored gelatin

2 tablespoons water

3 strips lemon zest, each about 3 inches long and ½ inch wide

1¼ cups sugar

⅓ cup all-purpose flour

2 large eggs

3 large egg whites

2¾ cups part-skim ricotta

8 ounces cream cheese

1 tablespoon lemon juice

2 teaspoons vanilla extract

Place oven rack just below the center of the oven. Preheat the oven to 350°F. Spray an 8-inch springform pan with nonstick spray.

With the metal blade in the workbowl, process the graham cracker pieces until coarsely crumbed, about 30 seconds. Place in the prepared pan and shake to coat the bottom and side. Discard excess.

Sprinkle the gelatin over the water in a microwave-safe custard cup. Let stand for a few minutes to soften. Microwave for 20 seconds at medium-high; stir to dissolve. Or dissolve gelatin by standing the custard cup in a small skillet of hot water over low heat on top of the range. Reserve.

Process the lemon zest and the sugar until the zest is finely chopped, about 60 seconds. Add the flour, the eggs, the egg whites, the ricotta,

(continued) ∼

*Nutritional information
per 3⅓-ounce serving:*

   calories 197

   fat 9.1g

   saturated fat 5.5g

   protein 8.2g

   carbohydrates 21g

   sodium 118mg

   cholesterol 55mg

Yield: 16 servings

*Nutritional information
per 3½-ounce serving:*

   calories 246

   fat 12g

   saturated fat 3.8g

   protein 5.7g

   carbohydrates 28g

   sodium 118mg

   cholesterol 56mg

the cream cheese, the lemon juice, and the vanilla; process until well-mixed, about 40 seconds. With the motor running, add 1 tablespoon of the reserved gelatin; process until the gelatin is incorporated, about 5 seconds. Discard the remaining gelatin. Pour the batter into the prepared pan and bake until the center is just firm and an instant-reading thermometer inserted in the center registers 165°F to 175°F, 50 to 70 minutes. Let cool completely in pan on a wire rack. Cover and refrigerate overnight. Before serving, remove the side of the pan.

VARIATIONS

Praline Cheesecake

Preheat the oven to 350°F. Toast 1 cup hazelnuts according to directions on page 34. Reserve.

To make the praliné, spray a 15½ by 10½ by ¾-inch baking sheet with nonstick spray. Combine 1 cup sugar with ¼ cup water in a heavy saucepan. Cook over moderately high heat, stirring only until the sugar has dissolved. Bring the mixture to a hard boil. Add the reserved hazelnuts and reduce heat to medium. Continue cooking, stirring occasionally with a wooden spoon, until the mixture turns golden brown. Quickly pour onto the prepared baking sheet; let cool and harden, about 1 hour.

Break the praliné into pieces that are no longer or wider than 2 inches.

With the metal blade in the workbowl, pulse to break the pieces to pea size, about 6 pulses; then process until very finely ground, at least 40 seconds. (The praliné should look powdered.) Reserve.

Now follow the Prize Cheesecake recipe, omitting the lemon zest and lemon juice and process the praliné powder along with the sugar, flour, eggs, egg whites, ricotta, cream cheese, and vanilla. Proceed with recipe as directed.

Apricot Cheesecake

In a small saucepan, cover 1 cup dried apricots (preferably Turkish or Australian) with cold water; simmer until soft, about 10 minutes. Drain apricots; puree with the metal blade until smooth, about 30 seconds. Reserve.

Follow the Prize Cheesecake recipe, omitting the lemon juice. Process the reserved apricot puree along with the flour, eggs, egg whites, ricotta, cream cheese, and vanilla. Proceed with the recipe as directed.

Yield: 16 servings

Nutritional information per 3¹⁄₃-ounce serving:
  calories 215
  fat 9.2g
  saturated fat 5.5g
  protein 8.5g
  carbohydrates 26g
  sodium 119mg
  cholesterol 56mg

Mocha Marble Cheesecake

Follow the Prize Cheesecake recipe, but omit the lemon zest and lemon juice and process the sugar along with the flour, eggs, egg whites, ricotta, cream cheese, and vanilla. After adding the gelatin and processing for 5 seconds, reserve the batter.

In a 1-quart microwave-safe bowl, microwave 3 ounces semisweet or bittersweet chocolate on high until soft, about 1 minute. Or melt the chocolate in a 1-quart heatproof bowl over hot water on top of the range. With a spatula, stir 2 teaspoons instant coffee granules into the chocolate. Gradually stir in 1 cup of the reserved batter. Reserve.

Transfer the remaining batter to the prepared pan: drop heaping tablespoonfuls of the reserved mocha batter (there will be about 9) over the surface, distributing them evenly. With a table knife, gently swirl the mocha batter into the plain batter. Bake and chill as directed in Prize Cheesecake recipe.

Yield: 16 servings

Nutritional information per 3¹⁄₂-ounce serving:
  calories 220
  fat 10g
  saturated fat 5.5g
  protein 8.5g
  carbohydrates 24g
  sodium 118mg
  cholesterol 56mg

Pound cakes made with cream cheese are popular with home cooks; chocolate chips give this version an extra attraction.

Yield: 20 servings

Nutritional information per 2¼-ounce serving:

calories 286 / 207
fat 18g / 8.4g
saturated fat 11g / 2.8g
protein 3.9g
carbohydrates 31g
sodium 84mg / 65mg
cholesterol 81mg / 25mg

CHOCOLATE CHIP POUND CAKE

1½ cups sugar

8 ounces cream cheese, cut into 16 pieces [or 9 ounces part-skim ricotta]

2 sticks unsalted butter, cut into 16 pieces [or ⅓ cup vegetable oil]

4 large eggs [or 2 large eggs and 3 large egg whites]

2 tablespoons sour cream [or ¼ cup water]

2 teaspoons vanilla extract

2¼ cups cake flour

2 teaspoons baking powder

¼ teaspoon salt (optional)

1 cup semisweet chocolate chips

Preheat the oven to 325°F. Prepare a 10-cup tube pan (9½ inches top diameter by 4 inches high) with nonstick spray.

To the workbowl with the metal blade, add the sugar, the cream cheese [or the ricotta], the butter [or the oil], the eggs [or the eggs and egg whites], the sour cream [or the water], and the vanilla; process until well mixed, about 20 seconds, scraping the bowl as necessary. Add the flour, the baking powder, and the salt; pulse until the flour just disappears, 3 to 5 times. Add the chocolate chips; pulse only until they are partly mixed in, 2 to 4 times.

Pour into the prepared pan; bake until lightly browned and a cake tester inserted in the center comes out clean, about 60 minutes. Let cool in the pan on a wire rack for 10 minutes; loosen around the side and tube with a small spatula; turn out onto rack to finish cooling.

SCOTCH POUND CAKE

~~~

¾ cup sugar

11 tablespoons unsalted butter, at room temperature, cut into 11
    pieces [or 3 tablespoons unsalted butter, at room temperature, and 7
    tablespoons unsalted margarine, cut into 10 pieces]

4 large eggs [or 2 large eggs, 2 large egg whites, and 2 tablespoons
    water]

2 tablespoons Scotch

1⅓ cups cake flour

¾ teaspoon baking powder

¼ teaspoon salt (optional)

Preheat the oven to 325°F. Spray an 8½ by 4¼ by 2½-inch (5-cup)
loaf pan with nonstick spray.

To the workbowl with the metal blade, add the sugar, the butter [or
the butter and margarine]; process until smooth, about 30 seconds, scraping the bowl as necessary. Add the eggs [or the eggs, egg whites, and
water] and the Scotch; process until well mixed, about 20 seconds,
scraping the bowl once. Add the flour, the baking powder, and the
salt; pulse until just combined, 4 to 6 times.

Pour into the prepared pan; bake until a cake tester inserted in the
center comes out clean, 55 to 60 minutes. Let cool in the pan on a
wire rack for 10 minutes; turn out onto rack to finish cooling.

*This unusual recipe of
James Beard's has a
mysterious, tantalizing
taste with universal
appeal.*

~~~~~~~

Yield: 10 servings

*Nutritional information
per 2½-ounce serving:*
   calories 265 / 240
   fat 12g
   saturated fat 15g / 3.9g
   protein 3.9g
   carbohydrates 28g
   sodium 28mg
   cholesterol 120mg / 52mg

Scented by rich dark rum and liberally laced with toasted pecans and apricots, this cake is a delicious accompaniment to midday, afternoon, or evening tea.

Yield: 10 servings

PECAN APRICOT POUND CAKE

½ cup pecans

1¾ cups all-purpose flour

¼ teaspoon salt (optional)

⅓ cup dried apricots

1 cup sugar

2 sticks unsalted butter [or 5 tablespoons unsalted butter and 11 tablespoons unsalted margarine], *cut into 16 pieces*

4 large eggs [or 2 large eggs, 2 large egg whites, and 2 tablespoons water]

1½ tablespoons dark rum

1 teaspoon vanilla extract

Rum Glaze (recipe follows)

Preheat the oven to 325°F. Spray a 6-cup ring mold (9½ inches top diameter and 2 inches high) with nonstick spray.

Spread the pecans on a baking sheet and bake until the nuts are lightly toasted, 6 to 8 minutes.

With the metal blade in the workbowl, process the flour, the salt, and the apricots until the apricots are finely chopped, about 45 seconds. Reserve.

Process the sugar and the butter [or the butter and margarine] until smooth, about 30 seconds, scraping the bowl once. Add the eggs [or the eggs, egg whites, and water], the dark rum, and the vanilla, and process an additional 30 seconds, scraping the bowl once. Add the pecans and pulse 2 times; add the apricot-flour mixture and pulse until just combined, about 4 times.

Pour into the prepared pan and bake until a cake tester inserted in the center comes out clean, 45 to 50 minutes. Loosen the side with a small spatula and turn out onto a wire rack and let cool. Drizzle the Rum Glaze over the cake before it cools completely.

RUM GLAZE

¹⁄₂ cup confectioners' sugar

1 tablespoon dark rum

¹⁄₂ teaspoon vanilla extract

2 tablespoons heavy cream [or 2 tablespoons 1% or skim milk]

With the metal blade in the workbowl, process all the ingredients until smooth, about 10 seconds.

VARIATION

~~~~~~

Pecan Pineapple Pound Cake

In place of the apricots use 2 whole slices dried, naturally preserved pineapple, quartered. Follow the directions for the Pecan Apricot Pound Cake, except process the pineapple and flour for 15 to 20 seconds.

Nutritional information per 3¾-ounce serving:

calories 440

fat 25g

saturated fat 13g / 7.1g

protein 5.7g

carbohydrates 47g

sodium 26mg

cholesterol 140mg / 62mg

Successful Techniques
for Freezing Cakes and Cookies

Cookies and cakes thawed after storage in a freezer sometimes have an off-taste or a soggy texture, but if you follow these suggestions we believe you will find them hard to distinguish from fresh-baked:

- Place cakes and cookies to be frozen (they may be glazed or frosted), unwrapped, in a single layer in the freezer for several hours, long enough to make them hard to the touch.
- Then place them in a single layer on a support such as cardboard covered with plastic wrap. If you stack layers, put plastic wrap between them.
- If the food is to be frozen for more than two days, wrap it in Saran Wrap®, enclosing it completely.* If it is to be used in a day or two, you may omit this step.
- Put the food in a plastic bag and squeeze out all the air you can. Squeeze the plastic together just above the food and twist to form the open side into a neck. Fold this neck double and secure it tightly with a twist tie. For best long-term protection, place the plastic bag inside another and seal it the same way. (If you use a zipper-type freezer bag, press out the air and seal the bag. Double-bag for long-term storage.)
- Thaw cakes and cookies at room temperature. Always let them thaw in their wrapping. If they are unwrapped while still frozen or very cold, moisture condensation from the air will make frostings runny and pastries soggy. Allow ample time for thawing—cakes may take a day, cookies several hours.

    Your freezer should maintain a temperature of 5°Fahrenheit or less. Checking periodically with a freezer thermometer, one with a horizontal liquid-filled glass tube, is a security precaution well worth taking.

---

*Protection against moisture transmission during freezer storage is important. Saran Wrap is the only readily available plastic film made of PVDC (polyvinylidene chloride), which provides four times as much protection as polyethylene. For evidence of this, cut an onion in half crosswise and wrap one half tightly in Saran Wrap, the other in some other plastic wrap; the odor comes through the other wrap more strongly.

Golden Layer Cake
page 18

Pain de Gênes
page 30

Applesauce Cake
page 37
Pineapple Upside-down Cake
page 45

Lemon Fancies
page 67

Pecan Pie Favorites
page 62

Classic Gingerbread
page 148

Christmas Roses
page 82

Maple Pecan Pie
page 98

Chocolate Chip Pound Cake
page 52

Williamsburg Orange Wine Cake
page 42

Lemon Sponge Roll with
Lemon Apricot Filling
page 23

Chocolate Mousse Surprise
page 162

ALL KINDS
OF COOKIES

PECAN PIE FAVORITES

HAZELNUT SQUARES

RAISIN BARS

SOUR CHERRY ALMOND SQUARES

LEMON FANCIES

LEGAL BROWNIES

CHOCOLATE PECAN REFRIGERATOR COOKIES

LEMON REFRIGERATOR COOKIES

FUDGE COOKIES

ALMOND DELIGHTS

PECAN SURPRISES

SWEDISH CRESCENTS

VANILLA ALMOND MACAROONS WITH MOCHA FILLING

LEMON SPRITZ COOKIES

CHRISTMAS ROSES

BROWN SUGAR SHORTBREAD PEOPLE

CHOCOLATE NUT BALLS

SESAME SEED COOKIES

FRESH GINGER COOKIES

SPICE PINE NUT COOKIES

All About Cookies

Cookies, as experienced cookie makers know, fall into five groups. Not one daunts the food processor.

Each of our *Cut-in-the-Pan Cookies* (except for our Legal Brownies) has a pastrylike bottom layer and an interesting topping or filling. Each is easy to prepare. We think you will enjoy the flavor variety they offer, from Pecan Pie Favorites to Sour Cherry Almond Squares.

For *Refrigerator Cookies,* the processor achieves a dough that is just the right consistency to chill, slice, and bake. We're proud of both our Lemon and our Chocolate Pecan Refrigerator Cookies, from a Canadian contributor, as well as of our other delicious recipes in this group.

Shaped Cookies usually call for few ingredients, which are processed instantly. Their dough is formed by hand into balls, crescents, ropes, or other shapes or put through a cookie press to produce a variety of designs. One example is Jim Beard's unusual Chocolate Nut Balls, shaped by hand. Fresh Ginger Cookies, proclaimed by our tasters to be "the best of their kind," are also shaped by hand. The recipe was contributed by cookbook author Marlene Parrish, whose food columns are well known to Pittsburgh newspaper readers. Another is Lemon Spritz, popular at holiday time, which calls for a cookie press.

Whether *Rolled Cookies* are sturdy or delicate, the processor handles their dough with speed and ease. Our Brown Sugar Shortbread People, designed to delight both children and grown-ups, are also delightfully easy to roll out and cut.

Mixtures for *Drop Cookies* are dropped onto baking sheets from a spoon or pastry bag. Those dropped from a spoon vary in texture, from thin enough to spread during baking to thick enough to keep their shape. Nina Simonds, an authority on Chinese food and a remarkably fine author, contributed her recipe for Spice Pine Nut Cookies—they are easy to process and easy to drop from a spoon. For our Vanilla Almond Macaroons, sandwiched together with a heavenly mocha filling, a pastry bag is used.

That's the overall picture. Because the food processor offers cookie makers the same shortcuts it offers cake makers, we suggest you read "Skipping Those Traditional, Tedious, Time-Consuming Cake-Making Steps," page 15.

The best tribute to these miniatures: All our tasters asked for the recipe.

Yield: 25 squares

Nutritional information per square, each about 1¼ ounces:

calories 166

fat 10g

saturated fat 3.5g / 1.3g

protein 1.8g

carbohydrates 18g

sodium 15mg

cholesterol 38mg / 8.5mg

PECAN PIE FAVORITES

1¾ cups pecan halves

1 cup all-purpose flour

¼ cup confectioners' sugar

1 stick plus 2 tablespoons unsalted butter [or 1 stick plus 2 tablespoons unsalted margarine], *cut into 10 pieces*

¾ cup firmly packed light brown sugar

½ cup dark corn syrup

1 teaspoon vanilla extract

¼ teaspoon salt (optional)

3 large eggs [or 1 large egg and 3 large egg whites]

Preheat the oven to 350°F. Spread the pecans on a baking sheet and bake until toasted, 6 to 8 minutes. Remove from the oven and reserve.

With the metal blade in the workbowl, process the flour, the confectioners' sugar, and 1 stick of the butter [or 1 stick of the margarine] until the mixture resembles coarse crumbs and just begins to hold together, about 15 seconds. Press into an ungreased 9-inch square pan and bake until firm and lightly colored, about 20 minutes.

Process the brown sugar and the remaining 2 tablespoons butter [or the remaining 2 tablespoons margarine] until creamy, about 10 seconds. Add the corn syrup, the vanilla, the salt, and the eggs [or the egg and egg whites]; process until combined, about 10 seconds, scraping the bowl once. Add the reserved pecans and pulse until coarsely chopped, 6 to 8 times. Spread the pecan mixture over the crust and bake until firm in the center, 35 to 40 minutes. Let cool in the pan on a wire rack.

Cut into 5 equal strips; give the pan a one-quarter turn and cut again into 5 equal strips to make 25 squares, each about 1¾ by 1¾ inches.

HAZELNUT SQUARES

1¼ cups toasted hazelnuts (see page 34)
*2 sticks unsalted butter, cut into 16 pieces [or 1½ sticks unsalted
        margarine, cut into 12 pieces]*
1 cup sugar
1 large egg yolk [or omit]
1¾ cups all-purpose flour
⅛ teaspoon salt (optional)
½ teaspoon ground cardamom
½ cup seedless raspberry jam

Preheat the oven to 275°F. Spray a 15 by 10 by ¾-inch jelly roll pan with nonstick spray.

With the metal blade in the workbowl, pulse the hazelnuts until pieces are rice-sized, 8 to 12 times; reserve. Process the butter *[or the margarine]*, the sugar, and the egg yolk until combined, about 25 seconds. Add the flour, the salt, and the cardamom. Pulse until well mixed, about 9 times.

Press the dough evenly over the bottom of the prepared pan. Spread the raspberry jam over the dough and sprinkle the reserved nuts evenly on top. Press the nuts lightly into place with your fingers. Bake until lightly browned around the edges, about 1 hour. Let cool in the pan on a wire rack. While still warm, cut into 12 equal strips from the 15-inch side and 8 equal strips from the 10-inch side to make 96 squares, each 1¼ by 1¼ inches. Let cool completely before removing from the pan.

The synergy between hazelnuts and raspberries creates a wonderfully vivid flavor combination.

Yield: 96 squares

Nutritional information per square, each about ⅓ ounce:

calories 51 / 45
fat 3.1g / 2.5g
saturated fat 1.3g / 0.3g
protein 0.5g
carbohydrates 5.5g
sodium 0.6mg / 0.3mg
cholesterol 8.0mg / 0

These pleasant,
satisfying cookies may
remind you of a treat
your grandmother made.
If you prefer your cookies
only moderately sweet,
reduce the sugar to
¼ cup.

Yield: 48 bars

RAISIN BARS

2½ cups raisins

½ cup sugar

½ teaspoon ground cinnamon (optional)

2 tablespoons cornstarch

¾ cup water

3 tablespoons lemon juice

1½ sticks unsalted butter [or 1½ sticks unsalted margarine], *cut into 12 pieces*

1 cup firmly packed dark brown sugar

1½ cups old-fashioned or quick-cooking oats

1½ cups all-purpose flour

½ teaspoon baking soda

½ teaspoon salt (optional)

Preheat the oven to 400°F. Spray a 13-by-9-by-2-inch pan with non-stick spray.

With the metal blade in the workbowl, pulse the raisins, the sugar, the cinnamon, and the cornstarch until the raisins are coarsely chopped, about 7 times. In a 2-quart saucepan over medium heat, cook the raisin mixture, the water, and the lemon juice, stirring constantly until thick, about 5 minutes. Remove from heat and let cool. Reserve.

Process the butter [or the margarine] and the brown sugar until creamy, about 20 seconds, scraping the bowl once. Add the remaining ingredients and pulse until just combined, 6 to 8 times. Divide in half.

Press half the oat mixture evenly over the bottom of the pan. Spread the reserved raisin mixture over it. Sprinkle with the remaining oat mixture and press lightly with your fingers. Bake until lightly browned, 20 to 30 minutes. Let cool in the pan on a wire rack. Cut into 8 equal strips from the 13-inch side and 6 equal strips from the 9-inch side to make 48 bars, each 1⅝ by 1½ inches.

Nutritional information per bar, each about 1 ounce:

calories 104

fat 3.1g

saturated fat 1.8g / 0.6g

protein 1.1g

carbohydrates 19g

sodium 34mg / 11mg

cholesterol 7.7mg / 0

These are good make-aheads because they need to be refrigerated overnight, after baking and before cutting. Sour cherry preserves make a fabulous filling, but they are hard to find: Seedless raspberry preserves substitute well.

~~~~~~~~~

Yield: 16 squares

Nutritional information per square, each about 1¼ ounces:

> calories 175
> fat 10g
> saturated fat 4.0g / 1.4g
> protein 2.2g
> carbohydrates 22g
> sodium 4.7mg
> cholesterol 16mg / 0

SOUR CHERRY ALMOND SQUARES
~~~

¾ cup blanched almonds
1 cup all-purpose flour
½ cup firmly packed light brown sugar
1 stick unsalted butter [or 1 stick unsalted margarine], *cut into 8 pieces*
¼ teaspoon vanilla extract
¼ teaspoon almond extract
½ cup sour cherry preserves

Preheat the oven to 350°F.

With the metal blade in the workbowl, pulse the almonds until pieces are rice-sized, 12 to 15 times. Remove ¼ cup of the chopped almonds from the bowl and reserve.

Add the remaining ingredients except for the preserves to the work-bowl and process until the mixture resembles coarse crumbs, about 20 seconds. Reserve ½ cup of the crumb mixture and evenly press the rest into an ungreased 9-inch square baking pan.

Process the preserves until smooth, about 15 seconds. Spread the preserves over the crust; sprinkle with the reserved crumb mixture and then with the reserved chopped almonds.

Bake until golden, 25 to 30 minutes. Let cool in the pan on a wire rack. Cover with foil and refrigerate overnight.

Cut into 4 equal strips, give the pan a one-quarter turn, and cut again into 4 equal strips to make 16 squares, each about 2 inches.

LEMON FANCIES

∼∼∼

¼ cup confectioners' sugar

1 cup all-purpose flour

5 tablespoons unsalted butter [or 5 tablespoons unsalted margarine], cut
    into 5 pieces

¾ cup granulated sugar

½ teaspoon baking powder

2 large eggs [or 1 large egg and 1 large egg white]

3 tablespoons lemon juice

Preheat the oven to 350°F.

With the metal blade in the workbowl, process the confectioners'
sugar, the flour, and the butter [or the margarine]; pulse until the mixture
resembles coarse crumbs, 4 to 7 times. Press over the bottom of an
ungreased 8-inch square pan and bake until firm and lightly colored,
about 20 minutes.

Process the remaining ingredients until well combined, about 5 seconds. Pour over the crust and bake until the top looks set, about 20
minutes. Let cool in the pan on a wire rack. While still warm, loosen
the sides with a small spatula and sprinkle with confectioners' sugar.
Chill for a few hours before cutting. Cut into 5 equal strips; give the
pan a one-quarter turn and cut again into 5 equal strips to make 25
squares, each about 1½ by 1½ inches.

*Our tasters all
proclaimed this a bar
cookie of award-winning
quality.*

∼∼∼∼∼∼∼∼

Yield: 25 squares

*Nutritional information
per square, each about ¾
ounce:*

calories 63

fat 2.3g

saturated fat 1.4g / .4g

protein 1.0g

carbohydrates 10g

sodium 5.0mg

cholesterol 20mg / 7.2mg

Cutting Up Like a Pro

If you want cut-in-the-pan brownies to look trim and professional instead of shaggy and homemade, cut them *out* of the pan. To do so, line their baking pan with a sheet of aluminum foil long enough to extend an inch or so beyond two opposite sides. After baking, place the pan on a wire rack, loosen the two unlined sides with a small spatula, and let cool. Chill briefly uncovered, or cover tightly with foil and chill as long as overnight. Lift the batch from the pan, using the extended foil, to a cutting board. Turn upside down and strip off the foil; turn right side up. With a sharp knife cut into squares. If you like, wrap individually in plastic wrap; this is a good way to keep the brownies moist.

LEGAL BROWNIES

1 cup walnut halves

1/2 cup all-purpose flour

1 cup sugar

1/2 cup cocoa

4 large egg whites

1 stick unsalted butter, cut into 8 pieces [or 1/3 cup vegetable oil and 1 tablespoon water]

1 teaspoon vanilla extract

Preheat the oven to 350°F. Spray an 8-inch square pan with nonstick spray.

Spread the walnuts on a cookie sheet and bake until lightly toasted, 6 to 8 minutes. Remove from the oven and reserve.

With the metal blade in the workbowl, process the remaining ingredients until smooth, about 10 seconds. Add the reserved walnuts and pulse until walnuts are coarsely chopped, about 5 times. Pour into the prepared pan; bake until the top looks set, about 30 minutes. Let cool in the pan on a wire rack. Cut into 4 equal strips; give the pan a one-quarter turn and cut again into 4 equal strips to make 16 squares, each 2 by 2 inches.

Cocoa and egg whites take the place of chocolate and whole eggs in America's classic brownie recipe, and oil may even be used instead of the traditional butter. Cholesterol watchers cherish these and call them legal.

Yield: 16 squares

Nutritional information per square, each about 1 1/3 ounces:

calories 163 / 153

fat 9.6g / 8.5g

saturated fat 3.9g / 0.6g

protein 2.7g

carbohydrates 17g

sodium 14mg / 13mg

cholesterol 15mg / 0

These cookies are mouth-watering and dandy to have on hand for emergencies. Both the uncooked dough and the baked cookies freeze well. For a super flavor change, use hazelnuts instead of pecans.

~~~~~~~~

Yield: 6 dozen cookies

Nutritional information per cookie, each about 1/3 ounce:

  calories 62
  fat 4.0g
  saturated fat 1.8g / 1.0g
  protein 0.5g
  carbohydrates 6.7g
  sodium 7.4mg
  cholesterol 7.9mg / 2.9mg

CHOCOLATE PECAN REFRIGERATOR COOKIES

~~~~

3 ounces semisweet chocolate, broken into pieces

1/2 cup pecan pieces

2 sticks unsalted butter [or 6 tablespoons unsalted butter and 10 tablespoons unsalted margarine], cut into 16 pieces

1/4 cup granulated sugar

1/2 cup firmly packed light brown sugar

2 1/3 cups cake flour

1/2 teaspoon baking soda

1/4 teaspoon salt (optional)

With the metal blade in the workbowl, process the chocolate until coarsely chopped, about 1 minute. Add the pecans and pulse until coarsely chopped, 4 to 6 times; reserve.

Process the butter [or the butter and margarine] and the sugars until creamy, about 1 minute, scraping the bowl as needed. Add the flour, the baking soda, and the salt; pulse to combine, about 5 times. Add the reserved chocolate-pecan mixture and pulse until just mixed, about 4 times.

Divide the dough in half and roll each half into a log 1½ inches in diameter. Wrap tightly in plastic wrap and refrigerate until firm, at least 2 hours.

Preheat the oven to 350°F.

Cut the logs into ¼-inch slices and arrange them about 1½ inches apart on ungreased baking sheets. Bake until golden brown, 10 to 12 minutes. Remove with a wide spatula to wire racks to cool.

LEMON REFRIGERATOR COOKIES

Zest of 1 medium lemon

1 cup sugar

2 sticks unsalted butter [or 6 tablespoons unsalted butter and 10 tablespoons unsalted margarine], *cut into 16 pieces*

2⅓ cups cake flour

½ teaspoon baking soda

¼ teaspoon salt (optional)

With the metal blade in the workbowl, process the lemon zest and the sugar until the zest is finely chopped, about 1 minute. Add the butter [or the butter and margarine] and process until creamy, about 1 minute, scraping the bowl once. Add the remaining ingredients and process until combined, about 10 seconds.

Divide the dough in half and roll each half into a log 1½ inches in diameter. Wrap tightly in plastic wrap and refrigerate until firm, at least 2 hours.

Preheat the oven to 350°F.

Cut the logs into ¼-inch slices and arrange them about 1½ inches apart on ungreased baking sheets. Bake until golden, 10 to 12 minutes. Remove with a wide spatula to wire racks to cool.

A *real winner. Easy to make and so delicious. They store well too.*

Yield: 6 dozen cookies

Nutritional information per cookie, each about ⅓ ounce:

calories 52
fat 3.0g
saturated fat 1.8g
protein 0.4g
carbohydrates 6.4g
sodium 6.9mg
cholesterol 7.9mg / 2.9mg

FUDGE COOKIES

~~~

This is a chewy cookie with rich chocolate flavor.

~~~~~~~~~~

Yield: 4 dozen cookies

Nutritional information per cookie, each about ½ ounce:

calories 59
fat 3.2g
saturated fat 1.1g
protein 0.6g
carbohydrates 8.2g
sodium 9.8mg
cholesterol 9.6mg / 0

½ cup [or 1⅓ cups] granulated sugar

3 ounces German sweet chocolate, cut into squares [or omit]

2 squares (1 ounce each) unsweetened chocolate [or 4 squares (1 ounce each)], broken into 4 to 8 pieces

½ cup firmly packed light brown sugar [or omit]

1 stick unsalted butter [or 1 stick unsalted margarine], cut into 8 pieces

1 large egg [or 1 large egg white]

1½ teaspoons vanilla extract

¾ cup plus 2 tablespoons all-purpose flour

½ teaspoon baking soda

¼ teaspoon salt (optional)

With the metal blade in the workbowl, process the granulated sugar for 1 minute. Add the sweet chocolate and the unsweetened chocolate and process until finely chopped, about 1 minute. Add the light brown sugar, the butter [or the margarine], the egg [or the egg white], and the vanilla. Process for 1 minute, scraping the bowl once. Add the remaining ingredients; pulse to combine, about 6 times. Wrap the dough in plastic wrap and chill for 2 to 3 hours; may be refrigerated overnight.

Preheat the oven to 375°F.

Form the dough into 1-inch balls and place on ungreased cookie sheets. Bake 8 minutes for chewy cookies, 9 minutes for crisper cookies. Remove with a wide spatula to a wire rack to cool.

ALMOND DELIGHTS

❦❦❦

2 sticks unsalted butter [or ½ stick unsalted butter and 1½ sticks unsalted margarine], *at room temperature and cut into 16 pieces*

½ cup confectioners' sugar

½ teaspoon almond extract

2 cups all-purpose flour

⅛ teaspoon salt (optional)

¼ cup blanched almonds

Chocolate Almond Filling (recipe follows)

Preheat the oven to 350°F.

With the metal blade in the workbowl, process the butter [or the butter and margarine], the sugar, and the almond extract until creamy, about 20 seconds, scraping the bowl once. Add the flour and the salt and pulse until the flour just disappears, about 8 times, scraping the bowl once.

Roll rounded half-teaspoonfuls of dough into balls. Place about 1½ inches apart on ungreased baking sheets. Bake until firm but not brown, 10 to 12 minutes. Remove with a wide spatula to a wire rack to cool. Leave the oven on at 350°F.

Spread the almonds on a baking sheet and bake until lightly toasted, 8 to 10 minutes. Remove from the oven and let cool. With the metal blade in the clean, dry workbowl, pulse the almonds until finely chopped, 6 to 8 times.

Spread about ½ teaspoonful of the Chocolate Almond Filling on the bottom of one cookie. Place another cookie, bottom side down, on the

Although these cookies taste scrumptious and look sophisticated, even a novice can make them easily and successfully.

❦❦❦❦❦❦❦

Yield: 42 cookies

(continued) ❧

*Nutritional information
per cookie, each about ¼
ounce:*

    calories 101
    fat 6.3g
    saturated fat 3.3g / 1.4g
    protein 1.0g
    carbohydrates 10g
    sodium 1.2mg / 0.6mg
    cholesterol 14mg / 2.9mg

filling and press lightly. Roll the chocolate edge of cookies in the reserved chopped almonds. Cookies can be stored in an airtight container for up to 2 weeks.

CHOCOLATE ALMOND FILLING

3 ounces semisweet chocolate, broken into pieces

2 tablespoons unsalted butter [or 2 tablespoons unsalted margarine]

2 tablespoons heavy cream [or 2 tablespoons water]

½ teaspoon almond extract

Pinch of salt (optional)

1 cup confectioners' sugar

With the metal blade in the workbowl, process the chocolate until finely chopped, about 1 minute.

In a small saucepan, over medium heat, bring the butter [or the margarine] and the cream [or the water] to a boil. With the motor running, slowly pour the hot mixture through the feed tube and process until the chocolate is smooth, about 15 seconds. Add the remaining ingredients and pulse 4 to 6 times to combine, scraping the bowl once. Use as directed.

PECAN SURPRISES

~~~

1¼ cups pecan pieces

1 cup all-purpose flour

2 tablespoons cornstarch

¼ teaspoon salt (optional)

2 sticks unsalted butter [or 6 tablespoons unsalted butter and 10 tablespoons unsalted margarine], at room temperature, cut into 16 pieces

1¼ cups confectioners' sugar

9 ounces milk chocolate, melted

1 teaspoon vanilla extract

Garnish: Pecan halves

Preheat the oven to 350°F. Spread the pecan pieces on a cookie sheet and bake until lightly toasted, 5 to 6 minutes. Remove from the oven and let cool. Turn the oven off.

With the metal blade in the workbowl, process the pecan pieces, the flour, the cornstarch, and the salt until the pecans are finely chopped, about 30 seconds. Reserve.

Process the butter [or the butter and margarine] and the sugar until creamy, about 20 seconds, scraping the bowl once. Add the melted chocolate and the vanilla and process until combined, about 10 seconds. Add the reserved flour mixture and pulse until the flour just disappears, 4 to 5 times. Refrigerate the dough for 1 hour.

Preheat the oven to 300°F. Roll slightly rounded teaspoonfuls of dough into balls and place on ungreased cookie sheets, about 2 inches apart. Lightly press a pecan half on top of each cookie. Bake until firm, 18 to 20 minutes. With a wide spatula, remove cookies to a wire rack to cool.

The subtle flavor of milk chocolate and an intertwining of pecans make these delicate cookies outstanding.

~~~

Yield: 9 dozen cookies

Nutritional information per cookie, each about ¼ ounce:

calories 49

fat 3.7g

saturated fat 1.1g / 0.6g

protein 0.5g

carbohydrates 4.0g

sodium 6.6mg / 2.1mg

cholesterol 4.6mg / 1.8mg

75

All Kinds

~

of Cookies

Chocolate Cookieholics, Please Note

Conventional recipes for chocolate cakes usually call for melting the chocolate over low heat or in the microwave, in a separate utensil. Our method of first chopping the chocolate in the workbowl, then heating one of the other ingredients such as butter or milk and pouring that through the feed tube works perfectly for cakes, but not always for cookies. The Pecan Surprises are a case in point:

When we followed the original recipe for these cookies, chopping the chocolate and pouring in melted butter, the dough after refrigeration seemed about the same as when the chocolate was melted in the microwave. But after baking, instead of emerging from the oven nicely rounded and tender, the baked cookies were flat, lacy, and chewy, with less flavor of blended chocolate and pecans.

The reason may be that cakes are baked in pans, which set their shape, whereas cookies are baked on a flat sheet. The cookie's shape depends on how far the dough spreads during baking, and that depends on the consistency of the dough and how it reacts to the oven heat. Melting the butter makes the dough for the Pecan Surprises spread too much, and this adversely affects the cookie's texture. So you may want to use caution when converting chocolate- or butter-cookie recipes to the food processor.

SWEDISH CRESCENTS

~~~~

1 cup pecan pieces

2 cups all-purpose flour

⅛ teaspoon salt (optional)

1 cup confectioners' sugar

1 tablespoon vanilla extract

1 tablespoon water

2 sticks unsalted butter, softened [or ½ stick unsalted butter, softened, and 1½ sticks unsalted margarine], *cut into 16 pieces*

Confectioners' sugar for coating

Preheat the oven to 350°F. Spread the pecans on a cookie sheet and bake until lightly toasted, 6 to 8 minutes. Remove from the oven and let cool. Turn off the oven.

With the metal blade in the workbowl, process the pecans, the flour and the salt until the nuts are finely chopped, about 30 seconds. Reserve.

Process the sugar, the vanilla, the water, and the butter [or the butter and margarine] until combined, about 20 seconds, scraping the bowl once. Add the reserved pecan mixture and pulse until it is just moistened, 8 to 12 times, scraping the bowl as necessary. Wrap the dough in plastic wrap and refrigerate for 1 hour or up to 1 week.

Preheat the oven to 325°F.

Form heaping teaspoonfuls of the dough into crescent shapes. Place about 1½ inches apart on ungreased baking sheets. Bake until firm but not brown, 12 to 15 minutes. Remove with a wide spatula to a wire rack to cool. While cookies are still warm, roll in the confectioners' sugar to coat.

Although this cookie classic was originally made with almonds, some Scandinavian-American families love the "melt-in-your-mouth" quality pecans contribute.

~~~~~~~~

Yield: 6 dozen cookies

Nutritional information per cookie, each about ⅓ ounce:

calories 52

fat 3.4g

saturated fat 1.6g / 0.8g

protein 0.5g

carbohydrates 5.0g

sodium 3.4mg / 3.9mg

cholesterol 6.4mg / 2.0mg

These are light, flavorful, and delicately crunchy. This recipe of Gaston LeNôtre's is the best of its kind we have ever found.

~~~~~~~~~

Yield: 40 filled cookies

Vanilla Almond Macaroons with Mocha Filling

~~~~

¾ cup blanched almonds

2 cups confectioners' sugar

4 large egg whites [or 4 tablespoons dried egg whites and 6 tablespoons water (see page 39)]

½ teaspoon vanilla extract

1½ tablespoons sugar

Mocha Filling (recipe follows)

Preheat the oven to 400°F. Line a large baking sheet with parchment paper and place another baking sheet under it.

With the metal blade in the workbowl, process the almonds and the confectioners' sugar until the almonds are finely ground, about 90 seconds, scraping the bowl as necessary. Reserve.

In a large mixing bowl, beat the egg whites [or the dried egg whites and water] with an electric mixer until soft peaks form. Add the vanilla; gradually beat in the granulated sugar, and continue beating, if necessary, until the whites are very stiff. With a spatula, gently fold the reserved almond mixture into the egg whites until well incorporated.

Put about half the mixture into a pastry bag with a ⅜-inch plain tube. Pipe 1-inch rounds of the mixture onto the prepared baking sheet, leaving about 1 inch between each round. Dip your finger in water and smooth the tops of the rounds. Bake on the double baking sheet in the center of the preheated oven for 4 minutes. Turn the baking sheets around and continue baking with the oven door partly open for about 4 minutes more, or until the tops of the macaroons are lightly browned and firm.

Slide the parchment sheet of macaroons onto a wire rack to cool. Repeat piping and baking with the remaining batter at once.

When all the macaroons are baked and cooled, remove them from the sheets of parchment with a wide spatula to a wire rack or tray. If the macaroons stick to the parchment paper, place the sheets on damp paper towels for about 1 minute to loosen, and then remove with the spatula.

The macaroons may be stored in airtight containers at room temperature for about a week. Or they may be frozen, appropriately wrapped, for a few months.

Fill the macaroons shortly before serving by lightly pressing the bottom half of each cookie with your finger to form a slight indentation or well. Spread about 1 teaspoon of the Mocha Filling on one indented macaroon and cover with an unfilled macaroon, pressing lightly together. Repeat with the remaining macaroons.

MOCHA FILLING

3 ounces white chocolate, broken into pieces
2 tablespoons unsalted margarine
2 tablespoons water
2 teaspoons instant coffee granules
1 cup confectioners' sugar
Pinch of salt

With the metal blade in the workbowl, process the chocolate until finely chopped, about 1 minute.

(continued) ~

Nutritional information per cookie, each about ¾ ounce:

  calories 70

  fat 2.5g

  saturated fat 0.2g

  protein 1.0g

  carbohydrates 11g

  sodium 7.8mg

  cholesterol 0.3mg

Put the margarine and the water in a small saucepan and bring the water to the boil. Remove from the heat and add the coffee, stirring to dissolve. With the motor running, pour the coffee mixture through the feed tube and process for 15 seconds, or until the chocolate is melted. Add the confectioners' sugar and the salt; process until smooth, about 20 seconds, scraping the bowl as necessary. Use as directed.

LEMON SPRITZ COOKIES

~~~

Zest of 1 small lemon

⅔ cup plus 2 tablespoons sugar

2 sticks unsalted butter [or 2 sticks unsalted margarine], cut into 16 pieces

2 teaspoons lemon juice

1 large egg

1 teaspoon vanilla extract

2½ cups all-purpose flour

¼ teaspoon baking powder

Pinch of salt (optional)

Garnish: 1½ bars (6 ounces) German sweet chocolate, cut into squares [or 2 tablespoons lemon juice and ½ cup confectioners' sugar]

Preheat the oven to 350°F.

With the metal blade in the workbowl, process the lemon zest and the sugar until the zest is finely chopped, about 1½ minutes. Reserve

Traditional holiday cookies you can have on hand in your freezer and garnish with a touch of glamour when you want to serve them.

~~~~~~~~

Yield: 9 dozen cookies

2 tablespoons of the lemon zest mixture for the garnish. Add the butter [or the margarine], the lemon juice, the egg, and the vanilla to the work-bowl and process until creamy, about 15 seconds, scraping the bowl as needed. Add the flour, the baking powder, and the salt; pulse until just combined, about 8 times.

Transfer the dough to a cookie press fitted with a 1½-inch-wide ridged disk. Press out strips onto an ungreased cookie sheet. With a sharp knife, cut strips at 1½-inch intervals, forming squares. Bake until firm but not brown, about 10 minutes. Remove with a wide spatula to a wire rack to cool, separating the cookies with the spatula.

To prepare and use the garnish

Melt the chocolate. Dip the cookies diagonally into the melted chocolate and sprinkle the chocolate with the reserved lemon zest mixture. Return to wire racks until the chocolate hardens.

[Or stir the lemon juice and the sugar until smooth. While the cookies are still warm, brush the top of each with the lemon juice mixture and sprinkle with the reserved lemon zest mixture. This gives a pretty, glazed effect.]

Nutritional information per cookie, each about ¼ ounce:

calories 42

fat 2.4g

saturated fat 1.1g / 0.3g

protein 0.5g

carbohydrates 5.0g

sodium 4.1mg / 1.6mg

cholesterol 6.6mg / 2.0mg

Yield: 3 dozen cookies

Nutritional information per cookie, each about $^{1}/_{3}$ ounce:

calories 45

fat 2.6g

saturated fat 1.6g / 0.5g

protein 0.5g / 0.4g

carbohydrates 4.7g

sodium 8.1mg / 0.3mg

cholesterol 12.6mg / 0

CHRISTMAS ROSES

$^{1}/_{4}$ cup confectioners' sugar

1 stick unsalted butter [or 1 stick unsalted margarine], cut into 8 pieces

1 large egg yolk [or omit]

$1^{1}/_{2}$ teaspoons vanilla extract

1 cup all-purpose flour

$^{1}/_{8}$ teaspoon salt (optional)

2 tablespoons currant jelly for piping

Preheat the oven to 350°F. Spray a cookie sheet with nonstick spray.

With the metal blade in the workbowl, process the sugar, the butter [or the margarine], the egg yolk, and the vanilla until creamy, about 15 seconds, scraping the bowl as needed. Add the flour and the salt and pulse until just combined, about 8 times.

Transfer the dough to a pastry bag equipped with a ½-inch star tip. Hold the bag upright over the cookie sheet and pipe out a star about 1¾ inches, then pipe a second, smaller star on the center of the first. Repeat the piping process with the remaining dough, leaving about 1½ inches between cookies.

Timesaving tip for a different shape: Transfer the dough to a cookie press fitted with a star-shaped disk. Press out cookies onto the prepared cookie sheet.

Bake until firm but not brown, 10 to 12 minutes.

Remove with a wide spatula to a wire rack to cool. When cool, put the currant jelly into a pastry bag fitted with a small plain tip and pipe a dab of jelly in the center of each cookie.

BROWN SUGAR SHORTBREAD PEOPLE

꙳꙳꙳

½ cup firmly packed dark brown sugar

2 sticks unsalted butter [or 2 sticks unsalted margarine], at room temperature, cut into 16 pieces

2½ cups all-purpose flour

⅛ teaspoon salt (optional)

With the metal blade in the workbowl, process the sugar and the butter [or the margarine] until creamy, about 20 seconds, scraping the bowl as needed. Add the flour and the salt; pulse until just combined, about 10 times. Divide the dough into thirds and wrap each piece in plastic wrap; refrigerate overnight.

Preheat the oven to 300°F.

On a lightly floured surface, roll out one portion of the dough at a time to ¼-inch thickness. With a floured 2-inch gingerbread cookie cutter, cut out the dough; with a wide spatula place the cutouts 1½ inches apart on ungreased baking sheets.

Bake until firm, 18 to 20 minutes. Remove with a wide spatula to a wire rack to cool. Decorate as desired.

These cookies look adorable and have great flavor and texture.

꙳꙳꙳꙳꙳꙳

Yield: 6 dozen

Nutritional information per cookie, each about ⅓ ounce:

    calories 46
    fat 2.6g
    saturated fat 1.6g / 0.5g
    protein 0.5g
    carbohydrates 5.2g
    sodium 4.6mg / 0.6mg
    cholesterol 7.1mg / 0

Toasted hazelnuts and semisweet chocolate, processed with three key ingredients, impart enticing flavor and engaging texture.

~~~~~~~~~~~~

Yield: 4 dozen cookies

Nutritional information per cookie, each about ⅓ ounce:

  calories 56
  fat 4.2g
  saturated fat 1.7g / 0.8g
  protein 0.8g
  carbohydrates 4.9g
  sodium 0.4mg / 0.2mg
  cholesterol 5.3mg / 0

CHOCOLATE NUT BALLS

~~~~

2 ounces semisweet chocolate, broken into 4 pieces

3 tablespoons sugar

1 cup toasted hazelnuts (see page 34)

1 cup all-purpose flour

1 stick unsalted butter [or 1 stick unsalted margarine], **at room temperature, cut into 8 pieces**

Confectioners' sugar for coating

Preheat the oven to 350°F.

With the metal blade in the workbowl, process the chocolate with the sugar until the chocolate is finely chopped, 30 to 40 seconds. Add the remaining ingredients and process until the mixture forms a ball, about 30 seconds.

Form slightly rounded teaspoonfuls of the dough into balls and place about 1 inch apart on ungreased baking sheets. Bake until firm, about 15 minutes.

Remove from the oven and let cool on cookie sheets for 3 to 5 minutes. Remove with a wide spatula to a wire rack and, while still warm, roll in the confectioners' sugar to coat.

Lard Is Better Than You Think

Long before the nutrition revolution, good pastry cooks used half lard and half butter in their piecrusts because the combination makes pastry both tender and flavorful. Lard was also used in cookies. We recommend it for Sesame Seed Cookies, page 87, and in the modified recipe for Spice Pine Nut Cookies, page 90.

In spite of the bad reputation of all animal fats today, lard and other animal fats are better for us than butter, according to the United States Department of Agriculture book *Composition of Foods.* Lard has about one third the cholesterol and less than two thirds the saturated fat content of butter. It also has more of the desirable monounsaturated fat than does butter. These are the Department of Agriculture's numbers:

	Butter	Lard
cholesterol*	256	95
saturated fat	62%	39%
monounsaturated fat	29%	45%

For a simple way to make your own pure lard, see page 86.

*milligrams per 100 grams

Making Food Processor Lard

Making lard is easy, and it is much better than the store-bought kind with its additives and preservatives.

To make ⅔ cup of lard, you'll need about a pound of pork fat. Fat from the outer side of pork chops or pork roasts is suitable; but if you can get fat from around the pork kidneys, do use it.

Chill the fat in the refrigerator until firm, cut it into pieces no larger than 1½ inches on a side. Chop them to pea size with the metal blade in the workbowl. Place in a 2-quart or larger microwave-safe bowl, add ½ cup water, cover loosely and cook at full power until the water boils, about 1½ to 3 minutes. Reduce the power to medium and cook, checking every 2 minutes, until all the water is evaporated and the melted fat just starts to change color at the edge. Use mitts to remove the bowl from the oven and let cool for 5 minutes.

Or place the fat with ¾ cup water in a 2-quart or larger saucepan over medium heat until the water comes to the boil. Reduce heat to low and cook, uncovered, until the fat just starts to sputter.

Pour through a fine strainer into a heat-resistant jar or crock. Cover and refrigerate. This will keep for at least 10 days in the refrigerator, and for months in the freezer if properly wrapped (see "Freezing Techniques," page 56).

Sesame Seed Cookies

2 cups all-purpose flour
¾ cup sugar
1 teaspoon baking powder
½ cup lard, at room temperature
1 large egg
2 tablespoons water
⅓ cup sesame seeds

With the metal blade in the workbowl, process all the ingredients, except the sesame seeds, until the mixture forms a ball, about 30 seconds. If the mixture does not form a ball, add an additional tablespoon of water and process 10 seconds more.

Divide the dough in half and roll each half into a log 1½ inches in diameter. Wrap tightly in plastic wrap and refrigerate until firm, at least 2 hours.

Preheat the oven to 350°F. Spray cookie sheets with nonstick spray.

Cut the logs into ¼-inch slices and arrange them about 1½ inches apart on the cookie sheets. Brush the slices with water and sprinkle evenly with the sesame seeds. Press down lightly to secure the seeds.

Bake until lightly browned and firm to the touch, 12 to 15 minutes. Remove with a wide spatula to wire racks to cool.

Sesame seeds add their attractive appearance and alluring flavor to these crisp cookies. This recipe was adapted from one by Jacques Pépin, world-renowned chef, author, and television host.

Yield: 4 dozen cookies

Nutritional information per cookie, each about ½ ounce:

calories 62
fat 3.0g
saturated fat 1.0g
protein 1.0g
carbohydrates 8.0g
sodium 2.0mg
cholesterol 6.4mg

Fresh Ginger:
Pleasingly Pungent in Cookies

Fresh ginger, light brown in color and gnarled, with aromatic and juicy flesh, is being put to good and increasing use in baking. Our Fresh Ginger Cookies, for example, gain their distinctive flavor from fresh ginger ground with sugar in the food processor.

A perennial question: What is the best way to store fresh ginger? Bruce Cost, author of *Ginger East to West* (Aris Books), says that fresh, firm ginger will last a week in the refrigerator if you just "toss it into the vegetable crisper." To store fresh, firm ginger in the refrigerator for 2 to 3 weeks, he advises putting it in "a plastic bag with a paper towel to absorb the moisture that can cause mold," or putting it in "a paper bag inside a plastic bag for the same effect."

Fresh ginger imparts its delightfully lively and piquant flavor to these firm but tender cookies.

Yield: 48 cookies

FRESH GINGER COOKIES

1 piece peeled fresh ginger, about 1 by 1 by 1/2 inch (See Note)

1 cup firmly packed dark brown sugar

1 1/2 sticks unsalted butter, at room temperature [or 3/4 cup lard, chilled], cut into 12 pieces

1/4 cup dark molasses

1 large egg

2 1/4 cups all-purpose flour

1 1/2 teaspoons baking soda

1/2 teaspoon salt (optional)

1/3 cup whole blanched almonds [or about 1 tablespoon sliced almonds]

With the metal blade in the workbowl, process the ginger and the sugar until the ginger is finely chopped, about 30 seconds, scraping the bowl as necessary. Add the butter [or the lard], the molasses, and the egg; process until well combined, about 30 seconds, scraping the bowl as necessary. Add the remaining ingredients except the almonds and pulse to combine, 3 to 5 times.

Wrap the dough in plastic wrap; refrigerate for at least 2 hours or overnight.

Preheat the oven to 350°F. Spray cookie sheets with nonstick spray.

Shape the dough into walnut-size balls; place 2 inches apart on the prepared cookie sheets. Press an almond [or an almond slice] in the center of each cookie. Bake until firm to the touch, 10 to 12 minutes. Remove with a wide spatula to a wire rack to cool.

For refrigerator cookies: Divide the dough in half and roll each half into a log 1½ inches in diameter. Wrap tightly in plastic wrap and refrigerate for at least 2 hours or overnight. Cut the logs into ¼-inch slices and arrange them about 2 inches apart on cookie sheets. Press an almond [or an almond slice] in the center of each cookie. Bake until firm to the touch, 10 to 12 minutes. Remove with a wide spatula to a wire rack to cool.

Note: If fresh ginger is not on hand, use 1 teaspoon ground ginger and add it along with the flour, baking soda, and salt.

Nutritional information per cookie, each about ½ ounce:

  calories 85

  fat 3.8g

  saturated fat 2.0g / 1.5g

  protein 1.1g / 0.8g

  carbohydrates 11g

  sodium 29mg

  cholesterol 12mg / 7.8mg

A *mellow blend of spices enhances these cookies, designed for snacking or to serve with fresh fruit as a simple supper dessert.*

Yield: 4 dozen cookies

SPICE PINE NUT COOKIES

2 sticks unsalted butter [or 6 tablespoons unsalted butter and 10 tablespoons unsalted margarine], *softened and cut into 16 pieces*

1 cup sugar

2 large eggs [or 1 large egg]

1½ teaspoons vanilla extract

2¼ cups all-purpose flour

1 teaspoon salt (optional)

½ teaspoon baking soda

1 teaspoon ground cinnamon

¼ teaspoon grated nutmeg

¼ teaspoon ground ginger

¼ teaspoon ground cardamom

¼ teaspoon ground allspice

Glaze: 1 large egg [or 1 large egg white] *lightly beaten with 1 tablespoon water*

½ cup pine nuts

Preheat the oven to 350°F. Spray cookie sheets with nonstick spray.

With the metal blade in the workbowl, process the butter [or the butter and margarine] and the sugar until creamy, about 1 minute. Add the eggs [or the egg] and the vanilla; process for 10 seconds. Add the flour, the salt, the baking soda, and the spices and pulse until combined, about 6 times.

Drop slightly rounded teaspoonfuls of the dough about 1 inch apart on baking sheets. Press the center of each cookie with your finger to form an identation or well. Brush with the egg glaze and press a few pine nuts into each identation. Bake until golden brown, 12 to 14 minutes. Remove with a wide spatula to wire racks to cool.

Nutritional information per cookie, each about ½ ounce:

calories 87

fat 5.1g

saturated fat 2.7g / 1.5g

protein 1.4g

carbohydrates 10g

sodium 12mg / 10mg

cholesterol 19mg / 8.3mg

TEMPTING PASTRIES

PINEAPPLE TARTLETS

MAPLE PECAN PIE

APRICOT, WALNUT, AND HONEY PIE

PEACH KUCHEN

BLUEBERRY RICOTTA TART

FRESH PEACH TART

SEPHARDIC LEMON TART

UPSIDE-DOWN PEAR TART

STRAWBERRY TART

BAKLAVA

PASTRY BRACELETS

One of the great features of the food processor is its ability to create, in excitingly brief time, the traditional and celebrated pastries of various countries.

To begin with, here are some of America's own special desserts: a ravishing Maple Pecan Pie, see page 98 for a note on it; a gorgeous Strawberry Tart of southern origin came to us from a Morristown, New Jersey, kitchen; and a Blueberry Ricotta Tart, originally developed by teacher and cookbook author Nicholas Malgieri—for our version of it, the food processor produces a light-in-calories but high-in-creaminess filling to offset a favorite American fruit.

Then there is the French pâte à chou (cream-puff pastry), valued in the United States for puffs to hold sweet or savory fillings. In France it has other uses. We have adapted one of them to the food processor to make delicious low-calorie shells for very special Pineapple Tartlets.

Another French recipe, for a suave Fresh Peach Tart, is the contribution of Lydie Marshall, who runs a cooking school in New York in the fall and winter and welcomes pupils to her château in France in the spring and summer. You'll never regret learning to make her lovely dessert.

A skillful variation of France's famous Tarte Tatin—Upside-down Pear Tart—is an outstanding accomplishment. It was created by Sally Darr, renowned American chef with a classic French background.

And from Alsace, his birthplace, comes André Soltner's Sephardic Lemon Tart, star dessert at Lutèce, famed New York restaurant.

Joyce Goldstein, much-traveled San Francisco restaurateur, brought back the recipe for La Buonissima—Apricot, Walnut, and Honey Pie—from Italy. It's just the sort of offering devotees of Italian desserts revel in.

We doubt that any food processor dessert has been more widely acclaimed than Peach Kuchen, of German vintage. Novelist and screen writer and director Nora Ephron even included a version of its recipe in her book *Heartburn*, from which the motion picture was made.

From the Middle East comes spectacular Baklava and Pastry Bracelets. With rich-in-nuts fillings processed in seconds and ready-made phyllo, these desserts can be part of the repertoire of ambitious home cooks.

Happy international pastry making!

Solving Pastry Problems

Even soft and sticky pastry and other short doughs are easy to roll out if you follow this suggestion:

Place a sheet of plastic wrap on the work surface and place the pastry in the center. Cover with another sheet of plastic wrap. Flatten the pastry into a disk and roll it out between the plastic sheets, which are easy to remove. For bread doughs and others that contain little or no fat, first spray the sheets of plastic wrap with nonstick spray.

Two suggestions in our recipes seem worth repeating here because they have general application:

Pastry recipes containing sugar tend to tear easily when rolled. To avoid the problem, prepare the pastry omitting the sugar, roll it out, then sprinkle the sugar evenly over the top and roll it in. It's much easier to work with and to handle, and the final result is the same. The recipe for Blueberry Ricotta Tart on page 104 gives this method.

The recipe for Strawberry Tart, page 112, gives an easy method for pressing a pastry dough into a pan and making it look smooth and professional: Place a sheet of plastic wrap over the dough and press it into place through the wrap, smoothing as you go.

These Pineapple
Tartlets are so luscious,
you may not be able to
resist calling them by
their French name—
Puits d'Amour, or Wells
of Love. Their shells,
created from cream-puff
dough, are much lower
in fat than the usual
shells made from pastry.

Yield: 3 dozen

PINEAPPLE TARTLETS

3 strips orange zest, each 3½ inches long and ½ inch wide

3 tablespoons sugar

⅓ cup water [or ⅔ cup water]

⅓ cup milk [or omit]

⅛ teaspoon salt (optional)

6 tablespoons unsalted butter [or 3 tablespoons unsalted butter and 3 tablespoons unsalted margarine]

⅔ cup all-purpose flour

2 large eggs [or 1 large egg and 2 large egg whites]

Pineapple Apricot Filling (recipe follows)

Garnish: Sweetened whipped cream (optional)

Preheat the oven to 400°F. Spray 3 dozen minimuffin cups with non-stick spray.

Put the zest and the sugar in a minichopper and process until zest is as fine as the sugar, about 20 seconds. Or hand-grate enough orange zest to make 2 teaspoons and mix well with the sugar.

In a 2-quart saucepan, over medium heat, place the zest mixture, the water, the milk, the salt, and the butter [or the butter and margarine]. When the butter melts and the liquids boil, remove from the heat; add the flour and stir with a wooden spoon until the mixture leaves the side of the saucepan. Return to low heat and cook for 2 minutes, stirring constantly. Remove from the heat and let this mixture (called *panade* in French) cool for 5 minutes.

To the workbowl with the metal blade, add the panade and the eggs [or the egg and egg whites]. Process until thick and shiny, about 30 seconds. Cover with plastic wrap and refrigerate for 15 minutes.

Place a teaspoonful of batter in each minimuffin cup. Dip your thumb in cold water and use it to spread the dough evenly over the inner surface of the cup. Place the filled minimuffin pans in the oven; reduce the heat to 375°F. Bake until medium brown, 18 to 20 minutes. Remove from the pans and let cool on wire racks.

Just before serving, fill each puff shell with a heaping teaspoonful of the chilled Pineapple Apricot Filling. If desired, garnish each filled shell with a rosette of sweetened whipped cream.

PINEAPPLE APRICOT FILLING

4 dried apricots

1 cup water

⅔ cup sugar

½ cup (4 ounces) drained unsweetened pineapple chunks

Pinch of salt (optional)

5 large egg yolks [or 1 large egg and 2 large yolks]

1 stick unsalted butter [or 3 tablespoons unsalted butter], **melted**

Simmer the apricots in 1 cup water, until soft, about 15 minutes; drain. With the metal blade in the workbowl, process the apricots with the sugar until pureed, about 30 seconds. Add the pineapple, the salt, and the egg yolks [or the egg and egg yolks]; process until smooth, about 40 seconds, scraping the bowl once. With the motor running, slowly pour the melted butter through the feed tube. Transfer the mixture to a 1½-quart saucepan or larger and cook over medium-low heat, stirring often, until very thick, about 15 minutes. Do not let boil. Put the mixture in a small bowl, cover tightly and refrigerate for at least one hour before using as directed.

Nutritional information per filled tartlet, each about 1 ounce:

calories 84 / 64

fat 5.6g / 3.4g

saturated fat 3.1g / 1.5g

protein 1.2g / 1.0g

carbohydrates 8.1g

sodium 6.5mg / 7.6mg

cholesterol 54g / 29g

As American as Maple Pecan Pie

When Americans want to describe something uncontestably American, we hold that the term should be "as American as Maple Pecan Pie." For this incredibly rich and lusciously sweet dessert originated in the United States and combines two foods indigenous to this country. The Indians taught the colonists to draw sap from sugar maple trees and make maple syrup. And our Native Americans showed early settlers where to find the deeply furrowed hickory trees that yield pecans. The word *pecan* comes from the Algonquin *paccan* and the Cree *pakan*. It's pronounced "pakan" or "peekan," depending on the section of the country you come from.

This fabulous dessert won first prize in a Maple Baking Contest in Chardon, Ohio, during an annual Maple Festival there. It was entered by Mrs. Nanci Jenkins of Ann Arbor, Michigan.

Yield: 8 servings

MAPLE PECAN PIE

Sour Cream Pastry (recipe follows)
1½ cups pecan halves, divided
½ cup sugar
2 tablespoons unsalted butter [or 2 tablespoons unsalted margarine], at room temperature
2 large eggs [or 1 large egg and 2 large egg whites]
2 tablespoons all-purpose flour
⅛ teaspoon salt (optional)
1 teaspoon vanilla extract
½ teaspoon cider vinegar
1½ cups pure medium-amber maple syrup

Prepare the Sour Cream Pastry and chill as directed.

Preheat the oven to 350°F.

Reserve 1 cup of the pecans for the top of the pie. Put the remaining ½ cup of pecans in the workbowl fitted with the metal blade and pulse until finely chopped, about 8 times; reserve.

With the metal blade in the workbowl, process the sugar and the butter [or the margarine] until combined, about 20 seconds, scraping the bowl as necessary. Add the remaining ingredients and the reserved chopped pecans; pulse until combined, about 5 times, scraping the bowl as necessary. Pour into the pastry-lined pie pan and arrange the pecan halves in concentric circles on top. Bake until the filling is set, 45 to 50 minutes. Let cool completely on a wire rack.

SOUR CREAM PASTRY

1½ cups all-purpose flour

¼ teaspoon salt (optional)

1 stick unsalted butter, chilled, [or 1 stick unsalted margarine, frozen], *cut into 8 pieces*

2 to 4 tablespoons sour cream [or 2 to 4 tablespoons ice water]

With the metal blade in the workbowl, pulse the flour, the salt, and the butter [or the margarine] until the consistency of coarse cornmeal, 6 to 8 times. Add the sour cream [or the water] and process until the dough holds together, about 30 seconds. Shape the dough into a 1-inch-thick disk, wrap in plastic wrap, and refrigerate for 1 hour.

On a lightly floured surface, roll the dough into a 12-inch circle; transfer to a 9-inch pie pan. Turn the overhang inside and flute the edge. Refrigerate until firm, about 30 minutes.

Nutritional information per 5-ounce serving:

calories 570 / 535

fat 30g / 28g

saturated fat 11g / 4.1g

protein 5.7g

carbohydrates 68g / 75g

sodium 26mg

cholesterol 87mg / 27mg

Walnuts star in both
the pastry and the filling
of this gratifying Italian
dessert.

〜〜〜〜〜〜〜〜

Yield: 10 servings

APRICOT, WALNUT, AND HONEY PIE

〜〜〜

Zest of 1 medium lemon

1 tablespoon sugar

¼ cup toasted walnut pieces (See Note)

1 cup all-purpose flour

½ stick unsalted butter [or 1 tablespoon unsalted butter and 3 tablespoons unsalted margarine], cut into 4 pieces

¼ teaspoon salt (optional)

2 tablespoons cold water

½ teaspoon vanilla extract

½ cup firmly packed dried apricots

2 tablespoons dark rum mixed with ¼ cup water

Walnut Honey Filling (recipe follows)

Put the lemon zest and the sugar in a minichopper: process until the zest is as fine as the sugar, about 20 seconds. Or hand-grate the zest fine and mix with the sugar.

With the metal blade in the workbowl, pulse the walnuts until finely chopped, 8 to 10 times. Add the flour, the lemon-sugar mixture, the butter [or the butter and margarine] and the salt; pulse until the consistency of cornmeal, about 6 times. With the motor running, add the cold water and the vanilla and process until the dough masses together. Shape the dough into a disk, wrap in plastic wrap, and refrigerate for 1 hour.

On a lightly floured surface, roll the dough into a 12-inch round; press evenly into a 10-inch tart pan with a removable bottom. Trim the dough, leaving a ½-inch overhang. Turn the overhang inside and press it into place around the edge of the pan. Refrigerate the crust until firm, about 30 minutes.

Preheat the oven to 425°F.

Line the pastry with aluminum foil and prick well with a fork. Bake for 12 minutes; remove the foil and continue baking until lightly browned, about 6 minutes. Let cool on a wire rack. Reduce the oven temperature to 325°F and place a baking sheet on the center rack.

In a small saucepan simmer the apricots, covered, in the rum-and-water mixture until soft, about 8 minutes; drain. With the metal blade in the workbowl, process the apricots until smooth, about 30 seconds, scraping the workbowl once. Spread the puree over the baked pastry and set aside.

Prepare the Walnut Honey Filling. Pour it over the apricot layer; place the pie on the baking sheet in the oven and bake until the filling is set, 35 to 45 minutes. Let cool completely on a wire rack.

WALNUT HONEY FILLING

1½ cups toasted walnut pieces (See Note)

¼ cup sugar

½ stick unsalted butter [or 1 tablespoon unsalted butter and 3 tablespoons unsalted margarine], **at room temperature**

½ cup honey

½ teaspoon ground cinnamon

5 large eggs [or 2 large eggs and 4 large egg whites]

2 teaspoons vanilla extract

¼ cup dark rum mixed with ¼ cup water [or 2 tablespoons dark rum mixed with ⅓ cup water]

In the workbowl with the metal blade, pulse the walnuts until coarsely chopped, about 6 times; reserve.

(continued) ~

Nutritional information per 3¾ ounce serving:

calories 410 / 380

fat 23g

saturated fat 7.5g / 4.0g

protein 7.5g

carbohydrates 42g

sodium 37mg

cholesterol 132mg / 49mg

Process the sugar, the butter *[or the butter and margarine]*, the honey, and the cinnamon until smooth, about 15 seconds, scraping the workbowl once. Add the eggs *[or the eggs and egg whites]*, the vanilla, and the rum-and-water mixture; process until well combined, about 10 seconds. Pulse in the reserved walnuts, about 2 times. Use as directed.

Note: To toast the walnuts, spread them on a cookie sheet and bake in a preheated 350°F oven for 6 to 8 minutes.

Measuring Honey and Molasses

These thick sweeteners are hard to pour and level off in a cup. Warming them in the microwave makes them much easier to handle. Remove the cap from the plastic or glass container and microwave the jar for 10 to 15 seconds on high. If necessary, repeat once or twice until the contents are easy to pour. A word of caution: These liquids absorb microwave energy quickly and will erupt, boiling, from the jar if overheated.

The contributor of this recipe describes it aptly. She says it makes "a summertime dessert that always wins compliments and pleas for more."

PEACH KUCHEN

1¼ cups all-purpose flour
¼ teaspoon salt (optional)
1 stick unsalted butter [or 3 tablespoons unsalted butter and 5 tablespoons unsalted margarine], cut into 8 pieces
2 tablespoons sour cream [or 2 tablespoons nonfat yogurt]
1½ pounds ripe peaches
Filling (recipe follows)

Spray a 9-by-1½-inch tart pan with a removable bottom with nonstick spray. Preheat the oven to 375°F.

Put the metal blade in the workbowl and add the flour, the salt, and the butter [or the butter and margarine]. Pulse until the mixture resembles coarse meal, about 4 times. Add the sour cream [or the yogurt] and process until the dough just begins to form a ball, about 10 seconds. Remove the dough and shape into a flat disk. Place the disk in the tart pan and press it out to evenly cover the bottom and side of the pan; bake until lightly browned, 18 to 20 minutes.

Let cool in the pan on a wire rack. Reduce the oven temperature to 350°F.

Peel and pit the peaches; cut them into ½-inch slices; set aside.

Make the Filling and pour ½ cup of it over the bottom of the baked crust. Arrange the peaches on top in concentric circles. Pour the remaining Filling evenly over the peaches. Bake until the top is lightly browned, 40 to 50 minutes. Cool for 10 minutes before removing side of pan. Serve warm or at room temperature.

FILLING

3 large egg yolks [or 1 large egg]

⅓ cup sour cream [or ⅓ cup part-skim ricotta]

1 cup sugar

¼ cup all-purpose flour

¼ teaspoon salt (optional)

With the metal blade in the workbowl, process the egg yolks [or the egg], the sour cream [or the ricotta], the sugar, the flour and the salt until combined, about 10 seconds, scraping the bowl as needed. Use as directed.

Yield: 8 servings

Nutritional information per 4¼-ounce serving:

   calories 365 / 340

   fat 17g / 13g

   saturated fat 9.6g / 4.7g

   protein 5.3g

   carbohydrates 52g

   sodium 12mg / 25mg

   cholesterol 117mg / 41mg

An inviting marriage
of the sweetness of the
cheese filling and the
tanginess of the berries.

BLUEBERRY RICOTTA TART

1 cup plus 2 tablespoons all-purpose flour

1/2 teaspoon baking powder

Pinch of salt (optional)

2 tablespoons unsalted butter, chilled and cut into 2 pieces

4 tablespoons unsalted margarine, chilled and cut into 4 pieces

1/4 cup cold water

3 tablespoons sugar

Ricotta Filling (recipe follows)

1 3/4 cups blueberries, washed and drained on paper towels

1 tablespoon all-purpose flour, mixed with 1 teaspoon ground
     cinnamon

Spray a 10-inch tart pan with a removable bottom with nonstick spray.

To the workbowl with the metal blade, add the flour, the baking powder, the salt, the butter, and the margarine. Pulse until the mixture resembles coarse cornmeal, about 4 times. Add the water and pulse until the dough just comes together, about 4 times. Shape the dough into a disk, wrap well in plastic wrap, and refrigerate for 1 hour.

On a lightly floured surface, roll out the dough to a 12-inch round. Sprinkle evenly with the sugar and roll the sugar in with the rolling pin. Fit into the tart pan, trimming the excess. Refrigerate for 30 minutes.

Preheat the oven to 400°F.

Line the pastry shell with foil and prick all over with a fork. Bake for 10 minutes. Remove the foil and continue baking until golden brown, about 5 minutes more. Remove from the oven and reduce the oven temperature to 350°F.

Make the Ricotta Filling.

In a large bowl, toss the blueberries with the flour-and-cinnamon mixture until they are well coated; add to the pastry shell. Pour the Ricotta Filling evenly over the blueberries. Bake until the filling is set, about 40 minutes. Cool in the pan on a wire rack.

RICOTTA FILLING

Zest of ¹/₂ medium lemon
¹/₄ cup plus 2 tablespoons sugar
1¹/₃ cups part-skim ricotta
1 large egg
2 large egg whites
1¹/₂ tablespoons flour
1 teaspoon vanilla extract

Put the zest and the sugar in a minichopper and process until the peel is as fine as the sugar, about 20 seconds. Or hand-grate the zest fine and mix it with the sugar.

To the workbowl with the metal blade, add all the ingredients and process until smooth, about 30 seconds, scraping the bowl once. Use as directed.

Nutritional information per 3¹/₂-ounce serving:
calories 235
fat 10g
saturated fat 4.0g
protein 7.1g
carbohydrates 30g
sodium 78mg
cholesterol 38mg

105
T e m p t i n g
P a s t r i e s

~~~~~

Perfect pastry and delicious fresh fruit flavor distinguish this attractive and satisfying dessert.

~~~~~~~~~

Yield: 8 servings

Pastry (recipe follows)
4 medium peaches, about 1¼ pounds
Lemon zest, 3 strips each, about 1 inch long by ½ inch wide
¾ cup sugar
2 tablespoons all-purpose flour
2 tablespoons lemon juice
2 large eggs [or 1 large egg, 1 large egg white, and 1 tablespoon water]

Prepare the pastry and bake as directed.

Peel and pit the peaches; cut them into ½-inch slices. Arrange the slices in concentric circles in the pastry.

With the metal blade in the workbowl, process the lemon zest with the sugar and the flour until the zest is finely chopped, about 1 minute. Add the lemon juice and the eggs [or the egg, egg white, and water]; process until well combined, about 15 seconds. Pour over the peach slices. Bake on a baking sheet until the filling is golden brown and set, about 30 minutes. Let cool on a wire rack for 30 minutes before removing the side of the pan. Serve warm or at room temperature.

PASTRY

1½ cups all-purpose flour
1 tablespoon sugar
Pinch of salt
1½ sticks unsalted butter, cut into 12 pieces [or 3 tablespoons unsalted butter and 5 tablespoons unsalted margarine, cut into 8 pieces]
3 tablespoons ice water

Preheat the oven to 400°F.

Spray a 9-by-1½-inch tart pan with a removable bottom with nonstick spray.

With the metal blade in the workbowl, pulse the flour, the sugar, the salt, and the butter [or the butter and margarine] until the consistency of coarse cornmeal, 6 to 8 times. Add the ice water and process until the dough holds together, about 30 seconds. Shape into a disk and wrap in plastic wrap; refrigerate for 30 minutes.

On a lightly floured surface, roll the dough into a 12-inch circle; fit the pastry in the tart pan. Line the pastry with aluminum foil, pressing it firmly, shiny side down, and prick well with a fork; bake for 15 minutes. Remove the foil and continue baking until golden brown, 6 to 8 minutes. Use as directed. Leave oven on at 400°F.

*Nutritional information
per 4-ounce serving:*
  calories 320 / 265
  fat 16g / 10g
  saturated fat 10g / 3.6g
  protein 4.0g
  carbohydrates 41g
  sodium 16mg
  cholesterol 86mg / 32mg

SEPHARDIC LEMON TART

~~~

Spanish Jews, whose forefathers settled in Alsace in the twelfth century, have always cherished this dessert. The Alsatian-born chef André Soltner, honored in both France and the United States for his outstanding work, prepares this fabled sweet so that it tastes the way his mother's did.

~~~~~~~~~

Yield: 12 servings

1 tablespoon all-purpose flour
1 cup almonds, blanched or unblanched
2 medium lemons
¾ cup sugar
3 large eggs, separated
Almond Meringue (recipe follows)

Preheat the oven to 350°F. Spray a 9-inch springform pan with non-stick spray.

With the metal blade in the workbowl, process the flour and the almonds until the almonds are finely chopped, about 90 seconds. Scrape the bowl as needed. Reserve.

Remove the zest from the lemons; reserve the lemons. (The zest of only 1 lemon is used for this recipe.) Process the zest of 1 lemon with ¼ cup of the sugar until the zest is finely minced, about 1 minute; reserve.

Process the egg yolks with the remaining sugar until light and lemon colored, about 1½ minutes. Transfer to a large mixing bowl. Stir in the reserved almond and lemon-zest mixtures.

In a large mixing bowl, beat the egg whites with an electric mixer until stiff peaks form. Add one quarter of the egg whites to the egg yolk mixture and fold in thoroughly. Fold in the remaining egg whites. Turn the mixture into the prepared pan and spread evenly with a spatula. Bake until firm in the center and lightly browned, about 30 minutes. Cool on a wire rack for 30 minutes. Remove the side from the pan and transfer to the center of a baking sheet. Set aside.

Make the Almond Meringue and reserve.

Remove the thick white pith from the reserved lemons, slice them with a very thin slicing disk, or by hand, so that the slices are wafer-thin. Remove any seeds. Arrange the slices in a single layer over the top of the tart. Spread with the reserved Almond Meringue. Make decorative lines on the meringue with a long spatula. Bake until the meringue is lightly browned, 15 to 20 minutes. Place on a wire rack and let cool before serving.

ALMOND MERINGUE

1/2 cup almonds, blanched or unblanched

2 large egg whites

1/4 cup sugar

With the metal blade in the workbowl, process the almonds until finely chopped, about 1 minute. Reserve.

Beat the egg whites until soft peaks form; add the sugar, 2 tablespoon-fuls at a time, beating for 10 seconds after each addition; continue beating until stiff peaks form. Fold in the almonds with a spatula. Use as directed.

Nutritional information per 2¼-ounce serving:

calories 190

fat 10g

saturated fat 1.2g

protein 5.8g

carbohydrates 22g

sodium 27mg

cholesterol 53mg

The sweet smoothness
of the pears combined
with the buttery caramel
flavor make this dessert
even richer-tasting than
the famous Apple Tart
Tatin.
〜〜〜〜〜〜〜

Yield: 4 servings

UPSIDE-DOWN PEAR TART
〜〜〜

Pâte Brisée Crust (recipe follows)
5 tablespoons unsalted butter [or 3 tablespoons unsalted butter]
7 tablespoons sugar [or 6 tablespoons sugar]
4 ripe but firm pears
2 tablespoons water (optional)
1 tablespoon sugar (optional)

Prepare the Pâte Brisée Crust and freeze as directed.

Spread 4 [or 2] tablespoons of the butter over the inside of a heavy, ovenproof 8-inch skillet with sloping sides. Sprinkle with 4 [or 3] tablespoons of the sugar. Peel, quarter, and core the pears. Reserve 1 quarter. Arrange as many quarters as will fit in a tight circle in the skillet, so that each has 1 straight side down and its rounded side is pointed up toward the side of the pan. Set aside any quarters that do not fit. Place the reserved quarter, rounded side down, in the center of the pears. Sprinkle 2 tablespoons of the remaining sugar over the pears in the skillet. Cook over medium-high heat, gently swirling the skillet as needed, until the sugar has caramelized to a rich golden brown, about 15 minutes.

Caramelize any leftover pear quarters in another small skillet, using the remaining 1 tablespoon butter and the remaining 1 tablespoon sugar (for both versions of the recipe). Place these quarters in the first skillet, filling any empty space and turning all the quarters rounded side down in the skillet.

Preheat the oven to 375°F and place a cookie sheet on the center rack. Bake the skillet of pears, uncovered, on the cookie sheet for 20 minutes. Remove the Pâte Brisée Crust from the freezer and invert over the pears; remove the waxed paper and continue baking until the crust is golden brown, 25 to 30 minutes.

Remove the skillet from the oven; swirl and shake over high heat for 1 to 2 minutes to evaporate the excess moisture and loosen any stuck caramel. Turn onto a wire rack with a serving dish under it. Cool on the rack for about 45 minutes and carefully slide onto a clean serving dish.

To make additional glaze for the top of the tart, add the optional 2 tablespoons water and the optional 1 tablespoon sugar to the skillet. Swirl the pan over high heat until the mixture is caramel colored and reduced to 1 to 2 tablespoons, about 2 minutes. Spoon over tart.

PÂTE BRISÉE CRUST

½ cup all-purpose flour

1½ teaspoons sugar [or 2 teaspoons sugar]

Pinch of salt

4 tablespoons unsalted butter, cut into 4 pieces [or 2 tablespoons unsalted butter, cut into 2 pieces, and 1 tablespoon vegetable oil]

1 tablespoon ice water

With the metal blade in the workbowl, pulse the flour, the sugar, the salt, and the 4 tablespoons butter [or the 2 tablespoons butter] until the consistency of coarse crumbs, 4 to 6 times. Add [the oil and] the water and pulse until the dough just comes together, about 4 times. Shape the dough into a 1-inch-thick disk, wrap in plastic wrap, and refrigerate for about 1 hour.

On a lightly floured surface, roll out the dough to a 9-inch round about ⅛ inch thick; carefully transfer the dough to a piece of waxed paper. Place an 8½-inch lid on the dough and cut around it with a sharp knife to fit the top of the skillet. With the point of a small knife, make a hole in the center of the crust to vent. Place the pastry round in the freezer for at least 1 hour. Use as directed.

Nutritional information per 7½-ounce serving:

calories 490 / 400

fat 26g / 18g

saturated fat 16g / 9.1g

protein 2.7g

carbohydrates 60g

sodium 4.4mg / 3.7mg

cholesterol 70mg / 40mg

So elegant and so
exceptionally good—it's
hard to believe it's so
easy to make.
~~~~~~~~

Yield: 8 servings

STRAWBERRY TART
~~~~

Short Crust Pastry (recipe follows)

[½ teaspoon gelatin]

1 tablespoon lemon juice

2 strips lemon zest, each about 3 inches long by ½ inch wide

½ cup sugar

3 ounces cream cheese [or 3 ounces Neufchâtel* cheese], quartered, at
    room temperature

1 cup heavy cream [or 1 cup whipping cream]

3 cups fresh strawberries, hulled

½ cup currant jelly

2 tablespoons kirsch or Triple Sec

Prepare and bake the Short Crust Pastry.

[If you are using the modified version of this recipe, sprinkle the gelatin over the lemon juice in a microwave-safe custard cup. Let stand a few minutes to soften. Microwave for 10 seconds on medium-high; stir to dissolve. Or dissolve the gelatin by standing the custard cup in a small skillet of hot water over low heat on top of the range. Reserve.]

With the metal blade in the workbowl, process the lemon zest and the sugar until the zest is finely chopped, about 30 seconds. Add the lemon juice [or the reserved gelatin–lemon juice mixture] and the cream cheese [or the Neufchâtel cheese]; process until smooth, about 20 seconds.

In a large mixing bowl, beat the cream with an electric mixer until thickened. Fold the cream-cheese mixture into the whipped cream and spoon into the crust; refrigerate for at least 4 hours.

*Neufchâtel is usually sold as a light cream cheese. It is a natural cheese with less fat than cream cheese.

Just before serving, decorate the top with the whole strawberries.

In a 1-quart saucepan over low heat, melt the jelly and stir in the kirsch or Triple Sec. Remove the pan from the heat and let cool for 5 minutes, stirring occasionally to prevent a film from developing. Spoon or brush the melted jelly over the strawberries to glaze.

SHORT CRUST PASTRY

1 cup all-purpose flour

1 stick unsalted butter, cut into 8 pieces [or 4 tablespoons unsalted butter, cut into 4 pieces, and 2 tablespoons vegetable oil]

3 tablespoons confectioners' sugar

Put all the ingredients in the workbowl fitted with the metal blade and process until the dough holds together, about 45 seconds. Shape into a disk and wrap in plastic wrap; refrigerate for 20 minutes.

Preheat the oven to 350°F. Spray an 8-inch springform pan with non-stick spray.

Press the dough roughly into the bottom of the pan, cover with a sheet of plastic wrap, and smooth out the dough until it evenly covers the bottom of the pan and extends about 1½ inches up the side; it should be about ¼ inch thick. Prick the dough with a fork and bake until golden brown, about 15 minutes. Let cool in the pan on a wire rack. Run a thin knife around the crust and remove the side of the spring-form pan.

Nutritional information per 5-ounce serving:

calories 405 / 340

fat 23g / 18g

saturated fat 14g / 11g

protein 3.5g

carbohydrates 45g

sodium 16mg / 64mg

cholesterol 70mg / 46mg

BAKLAVA

This innovative but authentic interpretation of a classic dessert is from a Chicago restaurateur with a Middle Eastern background.

Yield: 36 servings

4 cups walnut pieces

1 cup sugar

1 large egg

½ teaspoon ground cinnamon

Ground cloves

1 pound phyllo dough

4 sticks unsalted butter, **melted** [or nonstick, butter-flavored vegetable spray and 2 tablespoons unsalted butter, melted]

1 cup water

¼ cup honey (see page 102)

2 teaspoons lemon juice

Preheat the oven to 350°F. Spread the walnuts on a cookie sheet and bake until lightly toasted, 6 to 8 minutes. Remove from the oven and let cool. Reduce oven temperature to 325°F.

Spray a 9-inch square pan with nonstick spray.

Put half of the walnuts in the workbowl fitted with the metal blade; pulse until finely chopped, 8 to 10 times; reserve. Repeat with the remaining walnuts, leaving them in the workbowl. Add the reserved walnuts, ¼ cup of the sugar, the egg, the cinnamon, and a pinch of the ground cloves; pulse until just combined, 6 to 8 times.

Place the phyllo sheets in one pile on a smooth surface and with a sharp knife cut as many 9-inch squares as possible; cutting through all the layers of phyllo. Cut the scraps into 9-inch lengths. Cover the phyllo pieces with a damp towel to keep them from drying out.

[To prepare the modified version, spray the phyllo with butter-flavored vegetable spray instead of brushing with butter. Note: The top layer of the modified recipe is brushed with butter.]

Put a 9-inch phyllo square in the bottom of the pan and brush it with the melted butter. Continue, layering half of the 9-inch squares and brushing with butter. Then use half of the smaller phyllo pieces, brushing with butter.

When half of the phyllo leaves have been used, spread the nut mixture evenly over the entire surface. Continue layering the phyllo with the butter, using the smaller pieces first and finishing with the 9-inch squares on top.

Brush the top layer of phyllo generously with butter. With a sharp knife, score the top few layers with 6 vertical and 6 diagonal cuts, forming diamond shapes. Brush again with butter. Bake until golden brown, about 1 hour.

Prepare the syrup: In a small saucepan combine the remaining ¾ cup sugar, the water, the honey, the lemon juice, and a pinch of cloves. Bring to a boil over medium heat, stirring occasionally to dissolve the sugar. Reduce the heat to medium low and simmer until the syrup is reduced to about ½ cup, about 10 minutes. Reserve at room temperature.

Drizzle ¼ cup of the syrup over the top as soon as the Baklava has finished baking; let stand for 15 minutes and pour the remaining syrup over the top. Let stand at room temperature for at least 4 hours before cutting into diamond shapes and serving.

Nutritional information per 1¾-ounce serving:

calories 223 / 160

fat 17g / 9.0g

saturated fat 6.5g / 1.3g

protein 3.2g

carbohydrates 17g

sodium 43mg

cholesterol 30mg / 6.9mg

Crisp pastry and an
exotic-tasting filling
make these Middle
Eastern sweets extra-
special.

Yield: 30 servings

PASTRY BRACELETS

1 cup water

2½ cups sugar

2 drops rose water

2 cups walnut pieces

½ teaspoon ground cinnamon

8 ounces phyllo dough (15 sheets, each 16 by 12 inches)

1 stick unsalted butter, **melted** [or nonstick, butter-flavored vegetable spray and 2 tablespoons unsalted butter, melted]

To a 2-quart saucepan add the water and 2 cups of the sugar; bring to a boil over medium-high heat, stirring occasionally, until the sugar dissolves. Boil without stirring until a candy thermometer inserted in the sugar mixture registers 225°F (just below the syrup stage), about 6 minutes. Remove from the heat and stir in the rose water; let cool and reserve.

Preheat the oven to 350°F. Spread the walnuts on a cookie sheet and bake until lightly toasted, 6 to 8 minutes. Remove from the oven and let cool.

To the workbowl with the metal blade, add the walnuts, the remaining ½ cup sugar, and the cinnamon; pulse 4 times and then process until the walnuts are finely chopped, about 25 seconds.

Place the phyllo sheets in one pile on a smooth surface and with a sharp knife cut the stack once lengthwise and once crosswise into quarters. Place the quarters in one pile. Cover the phyllo with a damp towel to keep from drying out.

[To prepare the modified version, spray the phyllo with the butter-flavored vegetable spray instead of brushing with butter. Note: The modified coils are brushed with butter after being placed on the baking sheet.]

Using 2 sheets at a time, brush the top one lightly with butter and sprinkle evenly with 1 tablespoon of the walnut mixture. Roll the 2 sheets lengthwise around a chopstick and gently push in from both ends for a wrinkled effect. Carefully pull out the chopstick. Shape the pastry roll into a coil and place, seam side down, on a baking sheet and brush with butter. Continue shaping to make 15 coils, placing them against each other to prevent them from uncoiling during baking. Repeat with the remaining phyllo to make an additional 15 coils.

Bake until crisp and golden brown, about 15 minutes. With a wide spatula, slide the pastries onto wire racks. Place waxed paper under the racks to catch the drippings and spoon the reserved syrup over them. Let cool on the wire racks.

Nutritional information per 1⅓-ounce serving:

calories 138 / 150

fat 7.7g / 6.6g

saturated fat 2.2g / 1.0g

protein 1.8g

carbohydrates 21g

sodium 25mg

cholesterol 7.6mg / 1.8mg

GREAT
GO-ALONGS

RASPBERRY RICHES

PECAN COFFEE CAKE

DATE WALNUT RING

GARGANTAK
(AND ONE VARIATION)
Gargantak Braided Rolls

HONEY BRIOCHE

GRANDMA JUST'S STOLLEN

SWEDISH SWEET BREAD
(AND ONE VARIATION)
Lemon Raisin Coffee Cake

DANISH CREPES WITH APPLE FILLING

GOLDEN CREPES WITH PASTRY CREAM
AND A CHOICE OF SAUCES:
Raspberry Sauce
Chocolate Sauce

SCOTCH GINGERBREAD

CLASSIC GINGERBREAD

What to serve, other than a cake or cookies, as a go-along when you ask friends to come for coffee or tea over the weekend? The time may be morning, afternoon, or evening.

We suggest something not overly sweet. It may be, or become, a specialty of the house—nowadays called a signature dish.

Our go-alongs span a wide range. If you use a food processor when you bake with yeast, or if you would enjoy learning to do so, there are more than half a dozen recipes here to tempt you. Several are from two talented cookbook authors: America's favorite Pecan Coffee Cake and our version of her Date Walnut Ring from Anne Lindsay Greer, and two wonderful sweet Swedish loaves plus Honey Brioche from Suzanne Jones.

Then there is Gargantak (also called Cheoreg or Kahke), sent to us from Weymouth, Massachusetts, by a cook who adapted it from Rose Baboian's *The Art of Armenian Cooking*. This easy-to-prepare processor version is one to treasure.

For a nostalgic Christmas specialty, Grandma Just's Stollen is a fine choice. It came to us by a circuitous route: from a New York cook who tasted it in Mexico, where it was baked by Constantia Just, a grandmother of German descent who was born in Missouri. What could be more deliciously American?

For a change of pace there are Danish crepes with an irresistible apple filling and unusually tender golden crepes rolled around pastry cream and served with raspberry or chocolate sauce. Our testers and tasters gave both a very high rating. We hope you, too, will find them worthwhile.

Then there is Raspberry Riches—a cross between a quick bread and a cake that is named, with justification, after its seductive topping. It came to us from Shirley Sarvis, a talented food and wine consultant who lives in California.

Finally two great gingerbreads. A classic contribution from Craig Claiborne of *New York Times* fame and the author of many fine cookbooks. The other from Diana Kennedy, foremost authority on Mexican cookery, who still cherishes the British goodies she grew up with.

Each of these accompaniments for tea or coffee has its own engaging quality; each is designed to please.

The title says it: This coffee cake's topping of fresh raspberries, semisweet chocolate, and brown sugar is so sumptuous, it could have been invented by Midas.

~~~~~~~~~

Yield: 10 servings

RASPBERRY RICHES

~~~

Sugar Crumb Topping (recipe follows)
1 large egg
1/3 cup buttermilk
1/2 teaspoon vanilla extract
1/3 cup unsalted butter [or 1/3 cup unsalted margarine], melted and
    cooled to room temperature
1 cup all-purpose flour
3/4 cup sugar
1/2 teaspoon baking powder
1/4 teaspoon baking soda
1/4 teaspoon salt (optional)
1 pint fresh red raspberries

Make the Sugar Crumb Topping and reserve.

Preheat the oven to 375°F. Spray a 9-inch round cake pan with non-stick spray.

With the metal blade in the workbowl, process the egg, the buttermilk, the vanilla, and the butter [or the margarine] for 15 seconds. Add the dry ingredients and pulse until just combined, 3 to 4 times. The batter will be thick; spread evenly in the prepared pan and carefully place the raspberries on top. Sprinkle the reserved Sugar Crumb Topping over the raspberries.

Bake until a cake tester inserted in the center comes out clean, 35 to 40 minutes. Let cool in the pan on a wire rack. Serve warm.

Sugar Crumb Topping

½ ounce semisweet chocolate

½ cup firmly packed light brown sugar

2 tablespoons all-purpose flour

1 tablespoon unsalted butter, cut into 4 pieces

With the metal blade in the workbowl, process the chocolate until finely chopped, about 45 seconds. Add the remaining ingredients and process until well combined, about 20 seconds. Use as directed.

Nutritional information per 3-ounce serving:

calories 242

fat 8.8g

saturated fat 5.2g / 2.4g

protein 2.7g

carbohydrates 40g

sodium 54mg

cholesterol 42mg / 25mg

When Should That Coffee Cake
or Bread Come Out of the Oven?

Decades ago cookbook writers began advising their readers to tap or thump the bottom of a loaf of just-baked coffee cake or yeast bread with their knuckles and listen for the "hollow sound" that indicates proper doneness. While this procedure undoubtedly originated with experienced bread bakers, many cooks tell us that when they use this test, the legendary "hollow sound" just never emerges.

If you are interested in an up-to-date method for telling with certainty whether a loaf is done, we suggest the following:

Insert the stem of an instant-reading thermometer into the center of the loaf. If the reading is above 190°F, the coffee cake or bread is done. But remember this tip: Insert the thermometer stem vertically rather than at a slant. This way the hole left by the thermometer will be less apparent.

And a last word: When a loaf is fully baked it usually shrinks slightly from the pan.

PECAN COFFEE CAKE

~∾~

1 package dry yeast

1½ tablespoons sugar [or 2 tablespoons sugar]

¼ cup warm water (105° to 115°F)

⅓ cup cold milk [or ¾ cup cold skim or 1% milk]

2 large eggs [or omit]

3¼ cups all-purpose flour [or 2¾ cups all-purpose flour]

½ stick unsalted butter, cut into 4 pieces [or omit]

2 tablespoons unsalted margarine, cut into 2 pieces [or 3 tablespoons
   unsalted margarine, cut into 3 pieces]

1 teaspoon salt (optional)

¾ cup pecan halves [or ⅔ cup pecan halves]

Topping (recipe follows)

Spray the inside of a 1-gallon plastic food storage bag with nonstick spray.

In a 2-cup liquid measure, sprinkle the yeast and 1 teaspoon of the sugar over the warm water, stir to mix. Let stand until foamy, 5 to 10 minutes. Add the milk and the eggs.

Put the metal blade in the workbowl; process the flour, the remaining sugar, the butter, the margarine, and the salt for 20 seconds. With the motor running, pour the yeast mixture through the feed tube in a steady stream; stop the motor as soon as the dough forms a ball. Let rest for 3 minutes; process until the dough cleans the side of the bowl, 20 to 40 seconds.

(continued) ∾

*Y*ou can prepare this classic go-along at your own convenience because the dough needs refrigerating for 4 hours or for up to 4 days. The slow rising helps develop a fine, light texture.

~∾~∾~∾~∾~

Yield: 16 servings

*Nutritional information
per 2½-ounce serving:*

calories 271 / 201

fat 13g / 8.4g

saturated fat 5.3g / 1.9g

protein 4.6g / 3.4g

carbohydrates 35g / 29g

sodium 15mg / 8.6mg

cholesterol 46mg / 4.3mg

Put the dough into the prepared bag; twist the neck of the bag to remove the air and seal with a wire tie at the top of the bag. Refrigerate for at least 4 hours or for up to 4 days. Remove the wire tie and punch down the dough in the bag.

Spray a 9-inch round cake pan with nonstick spray.

Process the pecans until coarsely chopped, about 6 pulses. Reserve.

Prepare the Topping and spread over the bottom of the prepared pan. Sprinkle the reserved pecans over the Topping.

Divide the dough into 24 equal pieces and roll each into a smooth ball about 1¼ inches in diameter. Set the balls on the pecan mixture in 1 layer, leaving a little space between them. Cover with plastic wrap sprayed with nonstick spray and let rise in a warm place (70°F to 80°F) until doubled, about 1½ hours.

Bake in a preheated 350°F oven until lightly browned, 25 to 30 minutes. Cool in the pan for 5 minutes, then invert onto a serving plate. Scrape any remaining pecan mixture from the pan over the top of the coffee cake and let cool for at least 5 minutes before serving.

TOPPING

¾ cup firmly packed dark brown sugar [or ½ cup firmly packed dark brown sugar]

6 tablespoons unsalted butter, cut into 6 pieces [or 2 tablespoons unsalted butter and 2 tablespoons unsalted margarine, cut into 4 pieces]

¼ cup orange juice [or 3 tablespoons orange juice]

1 teaspoon vanilla extract

Process the brown sugar and the butter [or the butter and margarine] until smooth, about 20 seconds. Add the orange juice and the vanilla; pulse until combined, 6 to 8 times. Use as directed.

DATE WALNUT RING

~~~~

1 package dry yeast

2 teaspoons sugar

¼ cup [or 3 tablespoons] *warm water (105° to 115°F)*

¼ cup cold milk [or ½ cup skim or 1% milk]

1 large egg [or omit]

1¾ cups all-purpose flour

2 tablespoons unsalted butter, cut into 2 pieces

2 tablespoons unsalted margarine, cut into 2 pieces

1 teaspoon salt (optional)

¾ cup walnut pieces

Date Filling (recipe follows)

For spreading: 3 tablespoons unsalted butter [or 3 tablespoons
    unsalted margarine], softened

For brushing: 1 large egg [or 1 large egg white] *beaten with 1
    tablespoon water*

Confectioners' Sugar Glaze (recipe follows)

Spray the inside of a 1-gallon plastic food storage bag with nonstick spray.

In a 2-cup liquid measure, sprinkle the yeast and the sugar over the warm water, stir to mix. Let stand until foamy, 5 to 10 minutes; add the milk and the egg.

Put the metal blade in the workbowl; process the flour, the butter, the margarine, and the salt for 20 seconds. With the motor running, pour the yeast mixture through the feed tube in a steady stream; stop the

(continued) ~

This admirably textured coffee cake has a filling with few ingredients but extraordinarily rich flavor.

~~~~~~~~~~

Yield: 16 servings

*Nutritional information
per 2¼-ounce serving:*

calories 210

fat 10g / 8.9g

saturated fat 3.5g / 2.0g

protein 3.6g

carbohydrates 29g

sodium 10mg

cholesterol 40mg / 4.2mg

motor as soon as the dough forms a ball. Let rest for 3 minutes; process until the dough cleans the side of the bowl, 20 to 40 seconds.

Put the dough into the prepared bag; twist the neck of the bag to remove the air and seal with a wire tie at the top of the bag. Refrigerate for at least 4 hours or for up to 4 days. Remove the wire tie and punch down the dough in the bag.

Spray a 17-by-12-inch baking sheet with nonstick spray.

Preheat the oven to 350°F. Spread the walnuts on a cookie sheet and bake until lightly toasted, 6 to 8 minutes. Remove from the oven and let cool. With the metal blade in the workbowl, pulse the walnuts until coarsely chopped, 8 to 10 times; reserve.

Prepare the Date Filling.

On a lightly floured surface, roll the dough to a 15-by-7-inch rectangle. Spread the dough with the butter [or the margarine] and then the Date Filling to within ½ inch of the edge. Reserve 2 tablespoons of the walnuts and sprinkle the remaining walnuts over the Date Filling. Roll up tightly from a long edge and pinch the seam to seal. Transfer to the baking sheet and form into a ring. With a sharp knife, make an even number of cuts at 1-inch intervals, cutting within ⅛ inch from the bottom of the ring. Turn one section to the center, then the next to the outside of the ring, and continue until all of the sections are turned. Cover with plastic wrap sprayed with nonstick spray and let rise in a warm place (70°F to 80°F) until doubled, about 1½ hours.

Preheat the oven to 375°F. Brush the egg-water mixture over the top and sprinkle with the reserved 2 tablespoons walnuts; bake until golden brown, about 20 minutes.

Transfer to a wire rack to cool for 15 minutes. Place waxed paper under the rack to catch the drippings, then drizzle the Confectioners' Sugar Glaze over the top of the ring.

DATE FILLING

Zest of 1 small lemon
8 ounces chopped pitted dates
½ cup water

Put the zest in a minichopper and process until the peel is finely chopped, about 20 seconds. Or hand-grate the zest fine.

Put the dates, the water, and the lemon into a 1½-quart saucepan and cook over moderate heat, stirring often, until soft and thickened, about 15 minutes. Cool to room temperature and use as directed.

CONFECTIONERS' SUGAR GLAZE

½ cup confectioners' sugar
2 tablespoons heavy cream [or 2 tablespoons skim or 1% milk]
1 teaspoon dark rum

In a small bowl, whisk all the ingredients together until smooth. Use as directed.

No Armenian gathering would be considered festive without some version of *Gargantak*. No wonder! This bread, with its wonderfully light texture, is a great legacy. Here are directions for baking it in a handsome ring-shaped loaf or as fetching individual rolls.

Yield: 1 loaf, about 1¾ pounds

GARGANTAK

1 package dry yeast

3 tablespoons sugar

⅓ cup warm water (105° to 115°F)

2 large eggs [or 1 large egg and 2 large egg whites]

⅓ cup ice water

2¾ cups all-purpose flour

1¼ teaspoons baking powder (optional)

1 teaspoon salt (optional)

1 stick unsalted butter [or 2 tablespoons unsalted butter plus 6 tablespoons unsalted margarine], *melted*

Spray a 4-quart or larger bowl with nonstick spray.

In a 2-cup liquid measure, sprinkle the yeast and 1 teaspoon of the sugar over the warm water, stir to mix. Let stand until foamy, 5 to 10 minutes. Add the eggs [or the egg and egg whites] and the ice water.

To the workbowl fitted with the metal blade, add the remaining sugar, the flour, the baking powder, and the salt. With the motor running, pour the yeast mixture through the feed tube; stop the motor. Let rest for 3 minutes. Process for 15 seconds, and let rest 3 minutes more. Process the dough until it just cleans the side of the workbowl, 20 to 40 seconds. If the dough does not clean the side of the workbowl, add 1 tablespoon flour. With the motor running, add the butter [or the butter and margarine] through the feed tube and process only until it is combined; the dough will be soft.

Put the dough into the prepared bowl, and cover with sprayed plastic wrap. Let rise in a warm place (70°F to 80°F) until doubled, usually

1 to 1½ hours. Punch down the dough, cover tightly with sprayed plastic wrap, and refrigerate overnight.

Spray a 9-cup tube pan (9½ inches top diameter by 4 inches high) with nonstick spray. Punch the dough down again and shape it into a disk about 6 inches in diameter. Poke your thumb through the center and work the dough into a doughnut shape that fits into the bottom of the tube pan. Put into the prepared pan. Cover loosely with sprayed plastic wrap and let rise in a warm place until the dough rises slightly above the edge of the pan, usually 1½ to 2 hours.

Bake just below the center of a 375°F oven until golden brown and the loaf pulls away from the side of the pan, 35 to 40 minutes. Loosen around the side and the tube with a small spatula and turn out onto a wire rack to cool. Serve warm or at room temperature.

VARIATION

Gargantak Braided Rolls

Follow the recipe for Gargantak but after refrigerating overnight punch down the dough, then place it on a lightly floured surface and divide it into 12 equal portions. Working with 1 portion at a time, divide it into 3 equal pieces. Roll each piece into a thin, 10-inch-long rope. Press the 3 ends of the ropes together. Cross the rope on the right over the middle strip and bring the rope on the left over the middle rope. Continue braiding in this way, then press the ends together.

To shape a round braided roll, follow the above directions, then bring the two ends of the braid together, overlapping the ends ½ inch. Press to join the ends.

Spray baking sheets with nonstick spray and place the rolls, about 2 inches apart, on them. Let rise until doubled, usually 1½ to 2 hours. Bake in a preheated 375°F oven until golden brown, about 15 to 20 minutes.

Nutritional information per 1-ounce serving:

calories 92

fat 3.6g

saturated fat 2.2g / 1.0g

protein 2.1g

carbohydrates 13g

sodium 6.6mg

cholesterol 24mg / 10mg

Yield: 12 rolls, each about 2⅓ ounces

HONEY BRIOCHE

1 package dry yeast

3 tablespoons honey

¼ cup warm water (105° to 115°F)

2 large eggs [or 3 large egg whites]

1¾ cups all-purpose flour

¼ teaspoon salt (optional)

6 tablespoons unsalted butter [or 2 tablespoons unsalted butter and 4 tablespoons unsalted margarine], **melted**

Egg wash: 1 egg beaten with a pinch of salt

Spray a 4-quart or larger bowl with nonstick spray.

In a 2-cup liquid measure, sprinkle the yeast and 1 teaspoon of the honey over the warm water; stir to mix. Let stand until foamy, 5 to 10 minutes. Add the remaining honey and the eggs [or the egg whites].

To the workbowl with the metal blade, add the flour and the salt. With the motor running, pour the yeast mixture through the feed tube; stop the motor. Let rest for 3 minutes. Process for 20 seconds and let rest for 3 minutes more. With the motor running, add the butter [or the butter and margarine] through the feed tube and process only until just combined; the dough will be soft.

Put the dough into the prepared bowl, cover with sprayed plastic wrap. Let rise in a warm place (70°F to 80°F) until doubled, about 1 hour. Sprinkle 1 tablespoon additional flour on top of the dough and punch down. Cover tightly with sprayed plastic wrap and refrigerate overnight.

Spray a 6-cup ring mold (9½ inches diameter by 2 inches high) with nonstick spray. Punch down the dough and shape it into a disk about 6 inches in diameter. Poke your thumb through the center and work the dough into a doughnut shape that fits into the bottom of the ring mold. Put into the prepared pan. Cover loosely with sprayed plastic wrap and let rise in a warm place (70°F to 80°F) until the dough rises slightly above the edge of the pan, usually 1½ to 2 hours.

Brush the dough with the egg wash. Bake below the center of a pre-heated 425°F oven for 10 minutes. Reduce the heat to 350°F and bake for 8 to 10 minutes more, or until lightly browned. Loosen around the side and tube with a small spatula; turn out onto a wire rack; turn right side up with another rack. Serve warm or at room temperature.

Nutritional information per 1-ounce serving:

calories 104

fat 4.2g

saturated fat 2.7g / 1.4g

protein 2.3g

carbohydrates 14g

sodium 8.5mg

cholesterol 36mg / 3.8mg

Perfect to serve for a
holiday brunch, supper,
or other gathering, this
coffee cake is worth
including in a permanent
recipe repertoire.

Yield: 16 servings, each
about 3 ounces

GRANDMA JUST'S STOLLEN

1 package dry yeast

⅓ cup sugar

¼ cup warm water (105° to 115°F)

¼ cup plus 1 tablespoon cold milk [or ¾ cup ice water]

1 large egg [or omit]

1½ tablespoons brandy [or 2 tablespoons brandy]

1 teaspoon lemon juice [or omit]

3¼ cups all-purpose flour [or 3½ cups all-purpose flour]

1 teaspoon ground cardamom

¼ teaspoon salt (optional)

6 tablespoons unsalted butter [or 2 tablespoons unsalted butter and 4 tablespoons unsalted margarine], **cut into 6 pieces**

¼ cup mashed potatoes [or omit]

½ cup diced mixed candied fruit

¾ cup golden raisins

¼ cup currants

¼ cup sliced almonds

For brushing: 2 tablespoons unsalted butter [or 1 tablespoon unsalted margarine], **melted**

Sugar Glaze (recipe follows)

Spray the inside of a 1-gallon plastic food storage bag and a 17-by-12-inch baking sheet with nonstick spray.

In a 2-cup liquid measure, sprinkle the yeast and 1 tablespoon of the sugar over the warm water, stir to mix. Let stand until foamy, 5 to 10 minutes. Add the milk *[or ice water]*, egg, brandy, and lemon juice.

With the plastic dough blade in the workbowl, add the remaining sugar, the flour, cardamom, salt, butter *[or the butter and margarine]*, and mashed potatoes. With the motor running, pour the yeast mixture through the feed tube in a steady stream. Process until the dough forms a ball that cleans the side of the bowl; process 20 seconds more.

In a small mixing bowl, combine the candied fruit, the raisins, the currants, and the almonds. On a lightly floured surface, roll out the dough to a 12-by-8-inch rectangle; sprinkle with the fruit-and-nut mixture. Starting from a narrow edge, roll up tightly to distribute the mixture evenly and shape into a ball.

Put the dough into the prepared bag; twist the neck of the bag to remove the air and seal with a wire tie at the top. Let the dough rise in a warm place (70°F to 80°F) until doubled, usually 1½ to 2 hours. Remove the tie and punch down the dough in the bag. On a lightly floured surface, roll the dough into a 14-by-10-inch oval. Fold the long side over to within ¾ inch of the opposite side and press the top edge lightly to seal; curve the ends in to form a crescent. Place on the prepared baking sheet and cover loosely with sprayed plastic wrap; let rise again in a warm place until doubled, usually 1 hour.

Preheat the oven to 350°F.

Brush the stollen with the melted butter *[or the melted margarine]* and bake until golden brown, about 30 minutes. If the stollen browns too quickly, cover loosely with aluminum foil. Let cool on a wire rack; while still warm, drizzle with the Sugar Glaze.

SUGAR GLAZE

In a small bowl, whisk together 1 cup confectioners' sugar, 1 tablespoon brandy, and 1 tablespoon water until smooth.

Nutritional information per 3-ounce serving:

calories 255/ 245

fat 8.0g / 6.3g

saturated fat 4.0g / 1.7g

protein 4.0g

carbohydrates 42g

sodium 18mg / 2.8mg

cholesterol 30mg / 3.9mg

This loaf, with its
splendid flavor and
texture, has a beguiling
topping of sugar and
cardamom—the highly
aromatic spice so widely
used in holiday
specialties.

Yield: 26 servings

SWEDISH SWEET BREAD

1 package dry yeast

2 tablespoons sugar

¼ cup warm water (105° to 115°F)

1 teaspoon vanilla extract

¼ teaspoon almond extract

⅓ cup sour cream [or omit]

¼ cup milk [or ½ cup skim or 1% milk]

1 large egg [or omit]

3 cups all-purpose flour

½ stick unsalted butter [or 1 tablespoon unsalted butter and 3
    tablespoons unsalted margarine], *cut into 4 pieces*

½ teaspoon salt (optional)

Egg wash: 1 egg beaten with 1 tablespoon water [or 1 egg white
    beaten with 1 tablespoon water]

1 tablespoon sugar mixed with ¼ teaspoon ground cardamom

Spray the inside of a 1-gallon plastic food storage bag and an 8½ by
4½ by 2½-inch (6 cup) loaf pan with nonstick spray.

In a 2-cup liquid measure, sprinkle the yeast and 1 teaspoon of the
sugar over the warm water and stir to mix. Let stand until foamy, 5
to 10 minutes. Add the extracts, the sour cream, the milk, and the
egg.

With the metal blade in the workbowl, process the flour, the remaining
sugar, the butter [or the butter and margarine], and the salt for 20 seconds.
With the motor running, pour the yeast mixture through the feed tube
in a steady stream; process until the dough forms a ball that cleans
the side of the bowl; process for 20 seconds more.

Put the dough into the prepared bag. Twist the neck of the bag to remove the air and seal with a wire tie at the top. Let the dough rise in a warm place (70°F to 80°F) until doubled, usually 1½ to 2 hours. Remove the wire tie and punch down the dough in the bag; divide it into thirds. Shape each piece into a 12-inch strip. Carefully braid the strips without stretching them. Tuck the ends of the braid under and fit into the prepared pan. Cover loosely with sprayed plastic wrap and let rise again in a warm place until the dough rises slightly above the edge of the pan, usually 1 hour.

Bake in a preheated 375°F oven for 10 minutes, then remove from the oven and brush with the egg wash; sprinkle with the sugar-cardamom mixture. Continue baking until it is browned, 20 to 30 minutes more. If the loaf appears to be browning too quickly, cover loosely with aluminum foil. Turn out onto a wire rack and let cool.

Nutritional information per 1-ounce serving:
calories 92 / 83
fat 2.8g / 2.0g
saturated fat 1.6g / 0.6g
protein 2.1g
carbohydrates 14g
sodium 5.8mg / 2.8mg
cholesterol 15mg / 1.4mg

(continued) ↝

Yield: 12 servings,
approximately 2 ounces

*Nutritional information
per serving:*

    calories 248 / 227

    fat 6.2g / 4.2g

    saturated fat 3.6g / 1.2g

    protein 5.1g / 4.4g

    carbohydrates 43g

    sodium 14mg / 7.0mg

    cholesterol 32mg / 2.9mg

Lemon Raisin Coffee Cake

Follow the recipe for Swedish Sweet Bread, but add the zest of 1 medium lemon (see page 136) along with the flour. Proceed with the recipe until after the dough has risen. When you punch down the dough, knead in ½ cup golden raisins; shape into a 28-inch rope.

Starting in the center of a 9-inch round cake pan sprayed with nonstick spray, coil the rope loosely in the pan, tucking the end under securely. With kitchen scissors, snip the dough at 3-inch intervals about ¾ inch deep. Cover loosely with sprayed plastic wrap and let rise again in a warm place (70°F to 80°F) until risen slightly above the edge of the pan, usually 1 hour. Omit the egg wash and the cardamom-sugar mixture used in Swedish Sweet Bread.

Bake in a preheated 375°F oven until browned, 30 to 40 minutes. If the coffee cake seems to be browning too quickly, cover loosely with aluminum foil. Loosen the edge with a small spatula and turn out on a wire rack to cool. Place waxed paper under the rack to catch the dripping and, while slightly warm, drizzle with the following glaze:

¾ cup confectioners' sugar

1½ tablespoons milk [or water]

½ teaspoon vanilla extract

In a small bowl, whisk all the ingredients together until smooth.

Preheating Your Skillet

A skillet temperature of about 400°F is good for these low fat crepes. If the cooking surface is not hot enough, they will stick. If it is too hot, they will brown too fast.

To be sure that your skillet is properly preheated, gently sprinkle a few drops of water into it. If the temperature is about 400°F, the drops will break up into small spheres that roll around the pan before evaporating. If the temperature is too low, the drops of water will sputter and evaporate, but spheres will not form.

DANISH CREPES WITH APPLE FILLING

Apple Filling (recipe follows)

1 cup all-purpose flour

2 teaspoons sugar [or 1 tablespoon sugar]

3 large eggs [or 1 large egg and 3 large egg whites]

1½ cups milk [or 1½ cups skim or 1% milk]

2 tablespoons unsalted butter, melted [or 1 tablespoon vegetable oil]

Pinch of salt

1 tablespoon cognac

¾ cup sliced almonds

¾ cup seedless raspberry preserves

For broiling: 1 tablespoon sugar and 1 tablespoon cognac

Accompaniment: 1 cup heavy cream and 1 tablespoon cognac, whipped until stiff (optional)

You can make and fill these very thin pancakes ahead and heat them briefly just before serving.

Yield: 14 to 16 filled crepes

139

Great

Go-Alongs

(continued)

Nutritional information per crepe, each about 4 ounces:

    calories 300 / 200

    fat 19g / 6.8g

    saturated fat 9.8g / 2.1g

    protein 4.4g

    carbohydrates 32g

    sodium 25mg

    cholesterol 77mg / 20mg

Prepare the Apple Filling; cover and set aside.

With the metal blade in the workbowl, process the flour, the sugar, the eggs [or the egg and egg whites], the milk, the butter [or the oil], the salt and the cognac until smooth, about 20 seconds, scraping the bowl once. Transfer to a 4-cup measure.

Put 1 teaspoon of vegetable oil in a skillet with a 7-inch bottom. If necessary, wipe the bottom of the skillet with a paper towel to remove any excess oil. Place over medium heat until a few drops of water sprinkled in the pan form bubbles and evaporate. Lift the pan and pour in a scant ¼ cup of the batter; quickly rotate the pan so that the batter coats the bottom evenly, then return the skillet to medium heat. Sprinkle the top with a few almonds before the batter sets completely. Using a thin spatula, loosen the edge around the crepe to make sure it is lightly browned on the bottom; turn and cook until the almond side is lightly browned, about 30 seconds.

Invert the crepe onto waxed paper and repeat with the remaining batter. Spray a paper towel with nonstick spray; use it to wipe the bottom of the pan as needed.

The crepes can be made in advance and either refrigerated or frozen. Place a piece of plastic wrap between the crepes. If freezing, wrap the stack in plastic wrap.

Place the crepes, almond-side down, on a flat surface; spread 2 teaspoons of the raspberry preserves over each crepe. Spread 2 tablespoons of the Apple Filling on one half of each crepe. Fold each crepe in half, then in half again to form a fan.

Preheat the broiler.

Spray a shallow broiler-proof dish with nonstick spray. Arrange the crepes in the dish and sprinkle with the 1 tablespoon sugar and the 1 tablespoon cognac. The crepes may be made ahead to this point and kept, covered, for 2 to 3 hours at room temperature.

Broil the crepes 6 to 8 inches from the heat source until lightly browned, 1 to 2 minutes. Serve warm. Pass the whipped cream if you like.

APPLE FILLING

6 medium (about 2½ pounds total) Granny Smith apples
½ stick unsalted butter [or 2 tablespoons unsalted butter]
3 tablespoons lemon juice
½ cup sugar
½ teaspoon ground cardamom
½ teaspoon ground cinnamon

Peel, core, and quarter the apples; slice them with the medium slicing disk.

In a large saucepan over medium heat, melt the butter. Put the apples into the pan and stir; add the remaining ingredients and cook over low heat until the apples are tender, about 20 minutes, stirring occasionally. Use as directed.

Enjoy a Low-Calorie Filled Crepe

For a delicious crepe dessert that is really low in fat and calories, fill each crepe with 2 tablespoons Pear Frappé, page 181, and serve with 1 tablespoon Raspberry Sauce, page 144.

Nutritional information for each crepe:
    calories 95
    fat 2.6g
    saturated fat 0.6g
    protein 2.4g
    carbohydrates 16g
    sodium 21mg
    cholesterol 31mg

The delicate crepes, the creamy custard, the raspberry, and chocolate sauces—every part of this luscious dessert is make-ahead. Serve it with both sauces for a triumphant effect.

Yield: 16 to 18 crepes

GOLDEN CREPES WITH PASTRY CREAM AND A CHOICE OF SAUCES

Pastry Cream, recipe follows
Raspberry Sauce, recipe follows
Chocolate Sauce, recipe follows

GOLDEN CREPES

1⅓ cups skim or 1% milk
3 large eggs
2 tablespoons vegetable oil
½ teaspoon vanilla extract
1 cup all-purpose flour
½ teaspoon salt (optional)
1 tablespoon sugar
1½ teaspoons baking powder

Prepare the Pastry Cream and refrigerate until ready to use.

Prepare the Raspberry Sauce, if using, and refrigerate until ready to use.

Prepare the Chocolate Sauce, if using, and refrigerate until ready to use.

With the metal blade in the workbowl, process all the crepe ingredients until smooth, about 20 seconds, scraping the bowl once. Pour it into a 4-cup measure.

Put a teaspoon of vegetable oil in a skillet with a 5-inch-wide bottom. Wipe the bottom of the skillet, lightly, with a paper towel to remove any excess oil. Place over medium heat until a few drops of water sprinkled in the skillet form little globules before evaporating. Lift the skillet and pour in 2 tablespoons of the batter; quickly rotate the skillet so the batter evenly coats the bottom of the pan. Return the skillet to medium heat. Cook until the bottom is lightly browned, 30 to 60 seconds. Using a thin spatula, loosen the edge around the crepe and gently turn and cook about 20 seconds.

Invert the crepe onto waxed paper and repeat with the remaining batter. Spray a paper towel with nonstick spray; use it to wipe the bottom of the pan as needed.

The crepes can be made in advance and refrigerated or frozen with a piece of waxed paper or plastic wrap between the crepes. If freezing, wrap the stack in plastic wrap.

Spread the center third of each crepe with 2 tablespoons of the Pastry Cream. Fold each side over the filling and turn over. Serve with the Raspberry Sauce, Chocolate Sauce, or both.

PASTRY CREAM

1/3 cup sugar

1 tablespoon all-purpose flour

3 tablespoons light corn syrup

3 tablespoons cornstarch

1 large egg

2 cups 1% or skim milk

2 teaspoons unsalted butter

1 teaspoon vanilla extract

Nutritional information* per crepe:

calories 55

fat 2.5g

saturated fat 0.6g

protein 2.0g

carbohydrates 6.0g

sodium 17mg

cholesterol 31mg

*This takes into account that the first 3 or 4 crepes are generally unusable.

Yield: 2 cups

Nutritional information per tablespoon:

calories 24

fat 0.4g

saturated fat 0.2g

protein 0.3g

carbohydrates 4.5g

sodium 9.5mg

cholesterol 6.4mg

(continued)

To the workbowl with the metal blade, add the sugar, the flour, the corn syrup, the cornstarch, the egg, and ¼ cup of the milk; process until well mixed, 5 to 10 seconds. In a 2-quart saucepan over medium heat, bring the remaining 1¾ cups milk to just below the simmer. With the motor running, add about half the milk to the workbowl; process until well mixed, 5 to 10 seconds. Return to the saucepan and cook over medium-low heat, stirring constantly, until mixture thickens and starts to bubble. If not perfectly smooth, return to workbowl and process a few seconds. Remove from heat and stir in the butter and the vanilla. Let cool.

RASPBERRY SAUCE

1½ pints fresh raspberries, or 1 bag (12 ounces) frozen, unsweetened raspberries, thawed

½ cup sugar

2 tablespoons water

⅓ cup pure seedless raspberry jam

1 teaspoon framboise or himbeergeist (imported raspberry spirits), optional

Drain the raspberries; force them through a fine mesh strainer or put them through the power strainer of a food processor or a mixer to remove the seeds. In a small saucepan over medium heat, stir together the sugar and water just to dissolve the sugar. Put the raspberry puree, the sugar mixture, and the raspberry jam into the workbowl fitted with the metal blade and process until smooth, about 15 seconds. Taste, and if not sweet enough, process in more raspberry jam.

Covered and refrigerated, this sauce will keep for a week or more.

Yield: about 1½ cups

Nutritional information per 1 tablespoon serving:

calories 35

fat 0

saturated fat 0

protein 0.1g

carbohydrates 9.0g

sodium 0.5mg

cholesterol 0

Chocolate Sauce: How Thick? How Sweet?

Chocolate lovers are particular about the consistency and sweetness of Chocolate Sauce, and their preferences vary. Even small changes in the amount of water have a major effect on consistency; after making this recipe a few times, you'll know how much sugar and how much water are needed to suit your taste.

To cut chocolate squares easily, press down with the sharp point of a small knife. The chocolate will split under the knife point.

When you chop chocolate, watch the contents of the workbowl and listen. At the start you will hear the impact of the blade against the chocolate pieces, and you'll see the pieces bounce around in the workbowl. As the chopping proceeds, the sound changes. When it becomes almost even and there is only an occasional disturbance in the workbowl, the chocolate is chopped fine enough to melt when you pour in the hot liquid mixture.

CHOCOLATE SAUCE

This simple sauce is also delicious on ice cream. It may be varied by adding a little cognac, or coffee or orange liqueur, instead of the vanilla extract.

2 squares unsweetened chocolate, cut into pieces

¾ cup granulated sugar

¼ cup cocoa

⅓ cup water

1 tablespoon unsalted butter

1 teaspoon vanilla extract

In the workbowl with the metal blade, process the chocolate until finely chopped, about 30 seconds. Reserve.

Yield: 1 cup

Nutritional information per 1 tablespoon serving:

calories 57

fat 2.5g

saturated fat 1.1g

protein 0.6g

carbohydrates 10g

sodium 1.2mg

cholesterol 1.9mg

145

Great

(continued) *Go-Alongs*

In a small saucepan, whisk together the sugar and the cocoa until no lumps of cocoa remain; tilt the saucepan while whisking to incorporate the sugar and cocoa along the bottom edge. Gradually add the water, stirring with a wooden spoon until the mixture is smooth. Place the saucepan over medium heat and stir continuously across the bottom and sides until the mixture comes to the boil. Simmer 1 minute. With the motor running, slowly pour the hot mixture through the feed tube. Add the butter and the vanilla; continue processing until the sauce is smooth, about 20 seconds.

This sauce thickens as it cools. Tightly covered and refrigerated, it keeps for several weeks. Before use, warm gently to the desired consistency in a saucepan, stirring over low heat, or microwave for a few seconds at medium/low setting.

SCOTCH GINGERBREAD

~~~

1 cup firmly packed dark brown sugar (see page 45)

2 sticks unsalted butter, cut into 16 pieces [or ⅓ cup vegetable oil and
    ½ cup plus 2 tablespoons part-skim ricotta]

¾ cup dark molasses (see page 102)

2 large eggs [or 1 large egg and 1 large egg white]

⅓ cup milk [or ⅔ cup skim or 1% milk]

1⅔ cups all-purpose flour

1 teaspoon baking soda

2 tablespoons ground ginger

1 tablespoon ground cinnamon

Preheat the oven to 325°F. Spray a 13-by-9-inch pan with nonstick spray.

With the metal blade in the workbowl, process the sugar and the butter until smooth, about 1 minute, scraping the bowl once. *[If making the modified version, put the sugar, oil, and ricotta in the workbowl and continue with the recipe.]* With the motor running, pour the molasses, the eggs *[or the egg and egg white]*, and the milk through the feed tube; process until well combined, about 1 minute, scraping the bowl as needed. Add the remaining ingredients and pulse until they just disappear, 4 to 6 times.

Pour into the prepared pan; bake until a cake tester inserted in the center comes out clean, about 30 minutes. Let cool in the pan on a wire rack.

This recipe for "dark and sticky" gingerbread was published in a British newspaper almost fifty years ago and has been used by many people with great pleasure ever since.

~~~~~~~

Yield: 12 servings

Nutritional information per 2¾-ounce serving:
    calories 300 / *280*
    fat 14g / *7.9g*
    saturated fat 8.5g / *1.3g*
    protein 3.0g / *4.8g*
    carbohydrates 45g
    sodium 80mg / *109mg*
    cholesterol 66mg / *22mg*

We adapted this recipe, inspired by one of Craig Claiborne's, for the food processor. It's wonderful served alone or with applesauce or sweetened whipped cream.

~~~~~~~~

Yield: 12 servings

Nutritional information per 2-ounce serving:
calories 200 / 190
fat 8.8g / 7.7g
saturated fat 5.3g / 2.7g
protein 2.2g
carbohydrates 29g
sodium 80mg
cholesterol 40mg / 7.7mg

CLASSIC GINGERBREAD

~~~~

3 strips orange zest, each 3¹/₂ inches long by ¹/₂ inch wide

¹/₂ cup sugar

1 stick unsalted butter [or 3 tablespoons unsalted butter and 5 tablespoons unsalted margarine], cut into 8 pieces

1¹/₂ tablespoons sour cream [or omit]

¹/₂ cup molasses (see page 102)

¹/₄ cup water

1 large egg [or 2 large egg whites]

1¹/₄ cups all-purpose flour

1 teaspoon baking soda

1 teaspoon ground ginger

¹/₂ teaspoon ground cinnamon

¹/₄ teaspoon ground cloves

Pinch of ground nutmeg

Pinch of salt (optional)

Preheat the oven to 350°F. Spray an 8-by-8-inch pan with nonstick spray. With the metal blade in the workbowl, process the orange zest and the sugar until the zest is finely chopped, about 1 minute. Add the butter [or the butter and margarine]; process until smooth, about 1 minute, scraping the bowl once. Add the sour cream to the workbowl. With the motor running, pour the molasses, the water, and the eggs [or the egg whites] through the feed tube; process until well combined, about 1 minute, scraping the bowl as needed. Add the remaining ingredients and pulse until they just disappear, 4 to 6 times.

Pour into the prepared pan and bake until a cake tester inserted in the center comes out clean, about 35 minutes. Let cool in the pan on a wire rack.

Pleasing Puddings and Special Medleys

❧❧❧

BLUEBERRY CAROLE

BLUEBERRY CRISP

PEAR CLAFOUTIS

MRS. LINCOLN'S STRAWBERRY PUDDING

PRUNE SOUFFLÉ

TWO-WAY CHOCOLATE MOUSSE

CHOCOLATE MOUSSE SURPRISE

MOURÊMES AU CHOCOLAT

Our combinations of fruit and spice and all things nice make up a group of desserts we believe you will consider wonderfully worthwhile. Three of these desserts call for blueberries or strawberries. Two of them, Pear Clafoutis and Prune Soufflé, feature heartier fruits. They are perfect to serve to family and friends at informal lunches and suppers. And nowadays they are even used, on occasion, to end the most fashionable of dinners.

To crown this group, there are three chocolate medleys. You have our word for it that each is sensational and well suited to being conveniently made, as are the fruit desserts, in the food processor.

Strawberry Tart
page 112

Peach Kuchen
page 102

Grandma Just's Stollen
page 134

Blueberry Ricotta Tart
page 104

Pineapple Tartlets
page 96

Chocolate Pecan Refrigerator Cookies
page 70

Lemon Refrigerator Cookies
page 71

Sponge Cake with Hot Blueberry Sauce
page 21

Pastry Bracelets
page 116

Two-Way Chocolate Mousse
page 160

Ginger Ice Cream
page 184
Fresh Ginger Cookies
page 88

Sorbets
page 170

Fruit Frappés
page 177

BLUEBERRY CAROLE

～～～

2⅔ cups plus 3 tablespoons all-purpose flour

2 teaspoons salt (optional)

2 teaspoons sugar

2 sticks unsalted butter [or 5 tablespoons unsalted butter and 11 tablespoons unsalted margarine], cut into 16 pieces and frozen in separate portions

2 large egg yolks [or omit]

Ice water [or ½ cup ice water]

Crumb Topping (recipe follows)

2 large egg whites

2 pints fresh blueberries, washed and drained on paper towels

Spray a 15½ by 10½ by 1-inch jelly roll or cake roll pan with nonstick spray.

With the metal blade in the workbowl, process 2⅔ cups of the flour, the salt, the sugar, and the butter [or the butter and margarine] until the consistency of coarse meal, 8 to 10 seconds. If using the egg yolks, put them in a 1-cup measure and add enough ice water to make ½ cup. With the motor running pour the egg yolk and water mixture [or the ½ cup plain ice water] through the feed tube in a steady stream. Stop the machine as soon as the dough starts to hold together. Wrap the dough in plastic wrap and refrigerate for 1 hour. Press evenly into the prepared pan. Sprinkle with the remaining 3 tablespoons flour.

Preheat the oven to 400°F.

Prepare the Crumb Topping and reserve.

This dessert, a cross between a pudding and a tart, is the sort Americans love—fresh tasting, full of flavor, just substantial enough to satisfy, and foolproof to make. We find it as successful for casual entertaining as for more formal occasions.

～～～～～～

Yield: 16 servings

(continued) ～

*Nutritional information
per 3¼-ounce serving:*

calories 300

fat 15g

saturated fat 9.5g / 4.8g

protein 4.0g

carbohydrates 37g

sodium 11mg

cholesterol 63mg / 13mg

To the clean, dry workbowl with the metal blade, add the egg whites; process until they are stiff; their volume will not increase. With a spatula, in a large mixing bowl, gently fold the whites into the blueberries. Spread evenly over the dough, then sprinkle evenly with the Crumb Topping. Bake until the top is lightly browned, 35 to 40 minutes.

CRUMB TOPPING

1 cup all-purpose flour

1 cup sugar

1 stick unsalted butter [or 3 tablespoons unsalted butter and 5 tablespoons unsalted margarine], *cut into 8 pieces and frozen in separate portions*

Put the flour, the sugar, and the butter [or the butter and margarine] in the workbowl and process until the consistency of fine crumbs, 15 to 18 seconds. Use as directed.

BLUEBERRY CRISP

❧❧❧

3¾ cups fresh blueberries, washed and drained on paper towels

1 tablespoon plus 1 cup all-purpose flour

2 tablespoons plus ¼ cup granulated sugar

⅓ cup firmly packed light brown sugar

½ teaspoon ground cinnamon

1 stick unsalted butter [or 1 stick unsalted margarine], cut into 8 pieces

Preheat the oven to 375°F.

In a large mixing bowl, toss the blueberries with 1 tablespoon of the flour and 2 tablespoons of the granulated sugar until they are well coated. Place in an 8-inch square baking dish.

With the metal blade in the workbowl, process the remaining flour, the remaining granulated sugar, the brown sugar, and the cinnamon until well combined, about 10 seconds. Add the butter [or the margarine] and pulse until the mixture is the consistency of cornmeal, about 8 times. Sprinkle evenly over the blueberries.

Bake until the top is crisp and lightly browned, 40 to 45 minutes. Serve warm. Delicious topped with vanilla ice cream or vanilla frozen yogurt.

Quickly assembled, this dessert, with its fresh blueberries and cinnamon-scented topping, is one of summer's best rewards.

❧❧❧❧❧❧❧

Yield: 8 servings

Nutritional information per 3½-ounce serving:

calories 240

fat 10g

saturated fat 6.2g / 1.9g

protein 2.0g

carbohydrates 36g

sodium 6.5mg

cholesterol 27mg / 0

This particularly decorative version of a simple, old-time French dessert is from Madame Jeanette Pépin, mother of the well-known chef, teacher, and cookbook author, Jacques Pépin. On a visit to France, cookbook author Susan Purdy spent a few days with Madame Pépin in her charming house near Lyons and brought back the recipe for this very special clafoutis.

~~~~~~~~~

Yield: 8 servings

PEAR CLAFOUTIS

4 large ripe pears (about 2 pounds total)
6 to 7 tablespoons sugar
½ cup all-purpose flour
½ teaspoon baking powder
¼ teaspoon salt (optional)
3 large eggs [or 1 large egg and 2 large egg whites]
1 cup milk [or 1 cup skim or 1% milk]
1 teaspoon vanilla extract

If the pears are not ripe, steam them unpeeled, in a 4-quart saucepan with ½ cup water until they start to soften, 4 to 10 minutes. Remove from the heat and drain immediately.

Preheat the oven to 425°F. Spray a 10-by-1⅜-inch quiche or tart pan or a 10-inch cake pan with nonstick spray.

Peel the pears, slice them in half lengthwise, and remove the cores. Place each half, flat side down, on a cutting surface and cut crosswise into ⅛-inch slices. Slide the blade of the knife under each pear half and transfer to the pan with the stem end facing the middle. Repeat with the remaining pears, arranging them in a ring around the edge. Fan the pear halves toward the middle so that they cover the bottom of the pan. Sprinkle with 1 to 2 tablespoons of the sugar, depending on the sweetness of the pears.

With the metal blade in the workbowl, process 4 tablespoons of the sugar, the flour, the baking powder, the salt, the eggs [or the egg and egg whites], the milk, and the vanilla until smooth, about 15 seconds; pour over the pears. Sprinkle with 1 tablespoon sugar.

Bake for 15 minutes, then lower the oven temperature to 350°F. Continue baking until golden brown and a cake tester inserted in the center comes out clean, about 45 minutes more. Let cool on a wire rack. Serve while still warm.

Nutritional information per 6-ounce serving:

calories 170

fat 2.3g / 1.3g

saturated fat 0.6g / 0.3g

carbohydrates 36g

protein 4.2g

sodium 37mg

cholesterol 72mg / 27mg

*M*rs. A. D. Lincoln, *the first principal of the famous Boston Cooking School, used this delicious and unusual recipe in her 1883 cookbook. Today this unassuming dessert is delightful to serve for brunch.*

Yield: 6 servings

Nutritional information per 5¼-ounce serving:
  calories 240
  fat 12g / 9.2g
  saturated fat 6.6g / 1.6g
  protein 3.6g
  carbohydrates 35g
  sodium 3.3mg
  cholesterol 28mg / 0

158
P l e a s i n g
P u d d i n g s
a n d   S p e c i a l
M e d l e y s

MRS. LINCOLN'S STRAWBERRY PUDDING

Zest of ½ medium lemon
½ cup sugar
½ teaspoon ground cinnamon
6 tablespoons unsalted butter [or 4 tablespoons unsalted margarine], melted
1½ cups old-fashioned or quick-cooking rolled oats
2 pints fresh strawberries, hulled

Preheat the oven to 375°F. Spray a 6-cup soufflé dish with nonstick spray.

With the metal blade in the workbowl, process the lemon zest, the sugar, and the cinnamon until the zest is finely chopped, about 1 minute. Reserve.

In a small mixing bowl, stir the butter [or the margarine] into the oats. Reserve.

Slice the strawberries with the thick (6mm) slicing disk or ¼ inch thick by hand.

To assemble the pudding, put half of the oat mixture in the prepared soufflé dish. Top with half of the strawberries and half of the lemon-sugar mixture. Repeat the layering, ending with the lemon-sugar mixture. Bake until the top is lightly golden, about 45 minutes. Serve warm and, if you want to follow Mrs. Lincoln, with cream.

Prune Soufflé

～～～

16 whole, moist, pitted prunes (about ¾ cup)
2 tablespoons apple-flavored brandy, such as Calvados
¼ cup sugar
1 teaspoon lemon juice
4 large egg whites
⅛ teaspoon cream of tartar

Garnish: Confectioners' sugar

Place oven rack just below center of the oven. Preheat the oven to 350°F.

Spray a 6-cup soufflé dish with nonstick spray and sprinkle with granulated sugar.

With the metal blade in the workbowl, process the prunes, the apple brandy, the ¼ cup sugar, and the lemon juice until prunes are pureed, about 1½ minutes, scraping the bowl as necessary. Reserve in the workbowl.

In a large mixing bowl, beat the egg whites and the cream of tartar with an electric mixer until the whites are stiff but not dry. Add ¼ of the egg whites to the workbowl and pulse to combine, about 4 times. Add the remaining egg whites and pulse until just combined, about 4 times, scraping the bowl as necessary. Transfer the soufflé mixture to the prepared dish. Smooth the top with a rubber spatula and run your finger in a circle about 1 inch from the inside edge of the dish.

Place the dish in a deep baking pan and pour boiling water into the baking pan to come halfway up the side of the dish. Bake until golden brown and the center feels firm to the touch, about 30 minutes. Sprinkle with confectioners' sugar and serve immediately.

Rich in flavor and with a really satisfying texture, this dessert is deliciously low in calories and cholesterol.

～～～～～～～

Yield: 6 servings

Nutritional information per 2-ounce serving:

calories 110
fat 0.1g
saturated fat 0
protein 2.7g
carbohydrates 24g
sodium 34mg
cholesterol 0

This classic French
dessert has the virtue of
being made with egg
whites instead of whipped
cream. And it's two-way
because it can also be
baked and served as a
soufflé—as delicious,
either way, as you would
expect.

~~~~~~~~~

Yield: 12 servings

TWO-WAY CHOCOLATE MOUSSE
~~~

6 squares (1 ounce each) unsweetened chocolate, broken into
  pieces

1 cup sugar

⅓ cup boiling water [or ⅔ cup boiling water]

6 large eggs, separated [or 6 large egg whites]

¼ teaspoon cream of tartar

2 tablespoons strong brewed coffee or 1 teaspoon instant coffee
  granules dissolved in 2 tablespoons hot water

1 tablespoon vanilla extract

With the metal blade in the workbowl, process the chocolate and ½ cup of the sugar until the chocolate is finely chopped, about 1 minute. With the motor running, pour the hot water slowly through the feed tube and process until the chocolate is melted, about 1 minute. Reserve in the workbowl.

In a 3-quart or larger mixing bowl, beat the egg whites and the cream of tartar with an electric mixer until foamy. Beat in the remaining sugar by tablespoons, continue to beat, if necessary, until stiff peaks form.

Add the egg yolks, the coffee, and the vanilla to the melted chocolate; pulse until well-blended, about 4 times. Add ¼ of the egg whites to the workbowl and pulse to combine, about 4 times. Add the remaining egg whites and pulse until just combined, about 4 times. Scrape the workbowl as needed.

To serve cold, remove to a serving bowl or to individual dessert dishes. Refrigerate for several hours, until firm. To serve as a soufflé, transfer to twelve 6-ounce, ovenproof custard cups or ramekins. Preheat oven to 375°F. Place the filled cups on a baking sheet and bake until the tops are slightly puffed, 7 to 10 minutes. Serve immediately.

Nutritional information per 2⅓-ounce serving:

calories 174 / 145

fat 10g / 7.5g

saturated fat 0.8g / 0

protein 4.6g / 3.3g

carbohydrates 22g

sodium 29mg

cholesterol 107mg / 0

So delicious, it's
dreamy, this two-part
dessert—half firm and
cakelike, half soft and
creamy—delights all
tasters, chocoholic or not.
~~~~~~~~

Yield: 12 servings

CHOCOLATE MOUSSE SURPRISE
~~~~

12 ounces German sweet chocolate [or 9 squares (1 ounce each) unsweetened chocolate], broken into pieces

1 cup sugar [or 1½ cups sugar]

3 strips orange zest, each 3½ inches long by ½ inch wide (optional)

1½ sticks unsalted butter, melted and hot [or 1 cup boiling water]

9 large eggs, separated [or 8 large egg whites and 3 large egg yolks]

Pinch of salt (optional)

½ teaspoon cream of tartar

1 tablespoon orange liqueur, such as Grand Marnier [or 3 tablespoons brewed coffee and 1½ tablespoons vanilla extract]

1 cup whipping cream [or ½ cup whipping cream]

2 tablespoons confectioners' sugar

Garnish: Sweetened whipped cream and chocolate curls (optional)

Spray an 8-inch springform pan with nonstick spray. Preheat the oven to 350°F.

With the metal blade in the workbowl, process the chocolate, 1 cup of the sugar [the remaining ½ cup of sugar for the modified recipe is reserved for later use], and the orange zest until the chocolate is finely chopped, about 1 minute. With the motor running, pour the melted butter [or the boiling water] through the feed tube and process until the chocolate is melted, about 1 minute. Reserve in the workbowl.

In a 4-quart or larger mixing bowl, beat the 9 egg whites [or the 8 egg whites], the salt, and the cream of tartar with an electric mixer until foamy; continue beating [adding the remaining ½ cup of sugar by tablespoons] until stiff peaks form.

Add the 9 egg yolks [or the 3 egg yolks], and the orange liqueur [or the coffee and vanilla] to the melted-chocolate mixture; pulse until well blended, about 4 times. Add ¼ of the egg whites to the workbowl and pulse to combine, about 4 times. Fold the chocolate mixture gently but thoroughly into the remaining egg whites; spread half the mixture into the prepared pan (refrigerate the remaining chocolate mixture) and bake for 25 minutes. Remove the pan to a wire rack to cool.

Process the 1 cup whipping cream [or the ½ cup whipping cream] until slightly thickened, about 15 seconds. Add the confectioners' sugar and process until thicker, about 20 seconds. Fold gently but thoroughly into the remaining refrigerated chocolate mixture. Spread over the baked chocolate layer and freeze.

To serve, thaw in the refrigerator for 2 to 3 hours. Before serving, remove the side of the pan and garnish, if you like, with the whipped cream and chocolate curls.

Nutritional information per 4⅓-ounce serving:

- calories 450 / 270
- fat 33g / 16g
- saturated fat 19g / 7.1g
- protein 6.4g
- carbohydrates 35g
- sodium 59mg / 45mg
- cholesterol 220mg / 67mg

This is a rich dessert that some tasters think is the classical French custard called Pot de Crème, while others are sure it's a luscious mousse. Making it takes only minutes. It is a creation of Aileen Martin Berrard, the very gifted cooking-school teacher and restaurant consultant.

Yield: 6 servings

Nutritional information per 4¼-ounce serving:

calories 375
fat 25g
saturated fat 10g
protein 4.3g
carbohydrates 39g
sodium 38mg
cholesterol 125mg

164

P l e a s i n g
P u d d i n g s
a n d S p e c i a l
M e d l e y s

MOURÊMES AU CHOCOLAT

1 cup heavy cream
½ cup sugar
⅓ cup water
6 ounces semisweet chocolate, broken up
2 large eggs
½ teaspoon instant coffee granules
Pinch of salt
2 tablespoons Grand Marnier or coffee or hazelnut liqueur

Garnish: Sweetened whipped cream (optional)

In a 2-quart or larger mixing bowl, beat the heavy cream with an electric hand-held mixer until thickened.

To a 1-quart saucepan, add the sugar and the water; bring to a boil over medium-high heat, stirring just until the sugar dissolves.

With the metal blade in the workbowl, process the chocolate until finely chopped, 30 to 45 seconds. Add the eggs, the coffee, and the salt and process 5 seconds. With the motor running, pour the sugar syrup slowly through the feed tube and process until chocolate is melted and mixture is smooth, about 20 seconds, scraping the bowl once. Add the liqueur and process 10 seconds. Add the whipped cream to the workbowl and pulse until combined, about 4 times. Transfer the mixture to 6 ramekins and refrigerate overnight. Mixture will get very thick. If desired, garnish with sweetened whipped cream before serving.

∾∾∾

COOL
OFFERINGS

~~~

FRUIT SORBETS AND FROZEN FRUIT YOGURTS

FROZEN FRUIT FRAPPÉS

FROZEN BOMBES

GINGER ICE CREAM

SOUFFLÉ GLACÉ AUX FRAMBOISES
(FROZEN RASPBERRY SOUFFLÉ)

RASPBERRY ALMOND BAKED ALASKA

After a fully flavored or highly spiced main dish it is especially refreshing to serve a delicious fruit sorbet, frozen fruit yogurt, or fruit frappé for dessert—all made in record time in the food processor, all low in calories and fat. The fruit choices include bananas, peaches, pears, pineapple, blueberries, strawberries, and raspberries—either alone or in combination. Because you can use fresh fruit and some frozen fruit from your market in these frozen desserts, they fit into year-round menus.

For three different kinds of cool desserts we offer three other frozen delights. Ginger Ice Cream is a delicious homemade treat. Soufflé Glacé aux Framboises (Frozen Raspberry Soufflé) is a delectable and luxurious offering; it's from André Soltner, the famous chef-owner of New York's celebrated restaurant, Lutèce. Baked Alaska is a prestigious ending to a festive meal.

Frozen Fruit from Your Market for Frozen Desserts

Some fruits, most commonly strawberries, raspberries, and peaches, are available in frozen unsweetened form in your neighborhood market. When these fruits are not in peak season, the frozen variety is likely to have better flavor than the off-season fresh, because it is frozen shortly after picking. While these frozen fruits are often mushy when thawed, freezing has little effect on flavor. This makes them often a better choice than the fresh for sorbets, frozen yogurts, and frappés. Be sure to buy the unsweetened kind without syrup, usually packaged in bags; do not use the sweetened varieties, usually sold in boxes. Before processing, if necessary, cut all fruit into pieces of the size called for in the directions for making sorbets and frozen yogurts (see pages 170 and 174).

Keeping Fruit from Discoloring

For many years cooks have used lemon juice to keep apples, pears, and other fruits from turning brown after they are peeled or sliced. A simple, effective alternative is to stir ¼ teaspoon vitamin C powder into a pint of water. It dissolves instantly and does not affect the flavor of the fruit. Its generic name is ascorbic acid and it is sold in jars under several different labels in health food stores and drugstores. Some brands contain an added flavoring, so read the label to make sure you are getting pure ascorbic acid.

You'll find that it also prevents potatoes, eggplant, and similar vegetables from discoloring.

FRUIT SORBETS AND FROZEN FRUIT YOGURTS

~~~

These soft, refreshing frozen desserts are fat-free and low-calorie, with more fruit and much less sugar than usual recipes. Only minutes in the making, they can be served immediately or kept in the freezer for several hours.

You may further reduce the sugar content: Just substitute 1 packet aspartame sweetener for each tablespoon of sugar you omit, up to half the total amount. If the fruit you want to use is out of season, you may be able to buy the frozen variety; see the note on page 168.

The sorbet recipes yield about 1 pint, and the frozen yogurt recipes about 1½ pints. If your food processor bowl has a diameter greater than 6½ inches, you may double these recipes for a yield of about 1 quart.

Directions for Making Sorbets

At least 5 hours before serving, prepare the fruit—see the following Ingredient Listings for specifics. Cut the prepared fruit (except raspberries) into pieces no larger than 1 inch and freeze ¾ of it in a single layer. Refrigerate the remaining ¼ of the fruit. (Refrigerate ¼ of the seedless raspberry puree and freeze ¾ of it, flattened out in a gallon-size zipper-type plastic bag. Cut the frozen puree into 1-inch pieces before proceeding.)

A few minutes or up to 2 hours before serving, put half the frozen fruit into the workbowl fitted with the metal blade. Pulse a few times, then process to chop to pea-size, 20 to 60 seconds, depending on the hardness of the fruit. Empty the workbowl and reserve the contents. Put the remaining frozen fruit into the workbowl and chop to pea-size.

Add the refrigerated fruit pieces, the reserved pea-size fruit, the sweetening, and any additional ingredients called for in the Ingredient Listings. Process until the frozen mixture becomes creamy and circulates in the workbowl, scraping down the workbowl and the cover as necessary, about 30 to 90 seconds or more, depending on the fruit. Taste and, if needed, process in more sweetening. Serve immediately, or store in freezer for up to 2 hours.

Ingredient Listings

PEAR SORBET
~~~

3 large ripe pears (about 1½ pounds total), peeled and cored
½ cup confectioners' sugar
1½ teaspoons Williamine or other pear liqueur (optional)
¼ teaspoon vitamin C powder or 1 teaspoon lemon juice

Nutritional information per 4½-ounce serving:
calories 130
fat 0.5g
saturated fat 0

PEACH SORBET
~~~

1½ pounds ripe peaches, peeled and pits removed
½ cup confectioners' sugar
1 tablespoon peach schnapps

Nutritional information per 4½-ounce serving:
calories 110
fat 0.1g
saturated fat 0

(continued)

STRAWBERRY SORBET

~~~

1½ pints fresh strawberries (about 17 ounces total), washed and hulled

⅓ cup confectioners' sugar

1½ teaspoons fruit brandy, such as framboise or kirsch (optional)

PINEAPPLE SORBET

~~~

1 pound peeled and cored fresh pineapple, cut into 1-inch cubes (about 3 cups)

⅓ cup confectioners' sugar

1 teaspoon imported kirschwasser (optional)

RASPBERRY SORBET

~~~

2¼ pints fresh raspberries (about 23 ounces total), washed and forced through a strainer, or put through the power strainer of a food processor or a mixer, to yield about 2 cups seedless raspberry puree

½ cup confectioners' sugar

1½ teaspoons fruit brandy, such as framboise or kirsch (optional)

Small strawberries are preferable; they puree to a smoother consistency.

~~~

Nutritional information per 4½-ounce serving:

calories 78

fat 0.4g

saturated fat 0

Nutritional information per 4½-ounce serving:

calories 100

fat 0.5g

saturated fat 0

Nutritional information per 4½-ounce serving:

calories 118

fat 0.69g

saturated fat 0

Piña Colada Sorbet

~~~~~

1 pound peeled and cored fresh pineapple, cut into 1-inch cubes
   (about 3 cups)
¼ cup cream of coconut
1 teaspoon light rum

*So scrumptious, you'll
find it worth the 4.6
grams of saturated fat
and 107 calories in each
4½-ounce serving. Freeze
all the fruit, chop it, then
add the cream of coconut
and process until smooth.*

~~~~~~~~~

*Nutritional information
per 4½-ounce serving:*
   calories 110
   fat 5.7g
   saturated fat 4.6g

173
C o o l
O f f e r i n g s

Directions for Making Frozen Yogurts

Five hours or up to several days before serving, prepare the fruit—see the following Ingredient Listings for specifics. Cut the prepared fruit (except raspberries and blueberries) into pieces no larger than 1 inch and freeze them in a single layer. (Freeze the seedless raspberry puree flattened out in a gallon-size zipper-type plastic bag. Cut the frozen puree into 1-inch pieces before proceeding.)

A few minutes or up to 2 hours before serving, put half the frozen fruit pieces into the workbowl fitted with the metal blade. Pulse a few times, then process to chop to pea-size, 20 to 60 seconds, depending on the hardness of the fruit. Empty the workbowl and reserve the pea-size frozen fruit. Put the remaining frozen fruit pieces into the workbowl and chop to pea-size. Add the yogurt, the sweetening, the reserved pea-size frozen fruit and any additional ingredients called for in the Ingredient Listings. Process until the frozen mixture becomes creamy and circulates in the bowl; scraping down the workbowl and the cover as necessary, about 30 to 90 seconds or more depending on the fruit. Taste and, if needed, process in more sweetening. Serve immediately or store in freezer for up to 2 hours.

Frozen Pear Yogurt

❧

3 large ripe pears (about 1½ pounds total), peeled and cored
1 cup plain nonfat yogurt, very cold
⅔ cup confectioners' sugar
¼ teaspoon vitamin C powder or 1 tablespoon fresh lemon juice

Nutritional information per 6-ounce serving:

    calories 120

    fat 0.3g

    saturated fat 0

Frozen Strawberry Yogurt

❧

1½ pints fresh strawberries (about 17 ounces total), washed and hulled
1 cup plain nonfat yogurt, very cold
½ cup confectioners' sugar

Nutritional information per 6-ounce serving:

    calories 83

    fat 0.3g

    saturated fat 0

Frozen Blueberry Yogurt

❧

1 pound (2¼ cups) fresh blueberries, washed and stems removed
1 cup plain nonfat yogurt, very cold
½ cup confectioners' sugar

Nutritional information per 6-ounce serving:

    calories 100

    fat 0.3g

    saturated fat 0

(continued)

Nutritional information
per 6-ounce serving:

calories 100

fat 0.3g

saturated fat 0

Frozen Strawberry– Banana Yogurt

~~~~

1 banana (about 7 ounces), peeled

2¼ cups fresh strawberries, washed and hulled

1 cup plain nonfat yogurt, very cold

½ cup confectioners' sugar

Nutritional information
per 6-ounce serving:

calories 110

fat 0.4g

saturated fat 0

Frozen Raspberry Yogurt

~~~~

2¼ pints fresh raspberries (about 23 ounces total), washed and
    forced through a strainer or put through the power strainer of
    a food processor or a mixer, to yield about 2 cups seedless
    raspberry puree

1 cup plain nonfat yogurt, very cold

⅔ cup confectioners' sugar

Nutritional information
per 6-ounce serving:

calories 100

fat 0.1g

saturated fat 0

Frozen Peach Yogurt

~~~~

7 ripe medium peaches, about 22 ounces, peeled and pitted

1 cup plain nonfat yogurt, very cold

½ cup confectioners' sugar

Frozen Fruit Frappés

~~~~~~

It's fun to watch this intensely flavored, firm, creamy frozen treat expand more than four times as you whisk it. No one would guess how low-calorie it really is—many tasters assume it's a rich, delicious frozen mousse.

The fresh egg whites in these recipes can be replaced with the dried variety; see the note on page 39. With these, the amount of fruit can be increased by a third, from 6 ounces to 8, yielding an even more intensely flavored result.

These fruit frappé recipes yield about 1 pint. If your food processor bowl has a diameter greater than 6½ inches, you may double the recipes for a yield of about 1 quart.

Good News About Fruit Frappés

Even the most calorie- and fat-conscious can indulge themselves in fruit frappés—just look at the nutritional information for a full half-cup portion. Using dried egg whites for greatest fruit flavor adds less than 10 calories (22 calories for the Strawberry-Banana Frappé).

To save an additional 25 calories per serving, use 2 packets of aspartame sweetener instead of 2 tablespoons of sugar in any of these recipes.

Or, for a luscious special treat that is not a nutritional catastrophe, remove the frappé to a ½-quart or larger bowl, whip ½ cup whipping cream to soft peaks and fold it in. This "costs" 6 grams fat and 62 calories per ½ cup serving.

Basic Recipe for
Frozen Fruit Frappés

*6 ounces prepared fruit, frozen (or 8 ounces if using dried egg
   whites); see Ingredient Listings for choice of fruit*

1 large egg white (or 1 rounded tablespoon dried egg white)

3 to 5 tablespoons sugar, depending on sweetness of fruit

Fruit liqueur or spirits (where called for)

At least 5 hours before serving, prepare the fruit—see the following Ingredient Listings for specifics. Freeze in a single layer. (Freeze the seedless raspberry puree flattened out in a gallon-size zipper-type plastic bag. Cut the frozen puree into 1-inch pieces before proceeding.) Fifteen minutes or up to 2 hours before serving, chop the frozen fruit fine with the metal blade, scraping down the top and side of the workbowl as necessary. The fruit should look somewhat like powdered ice.

If Your Food Processor Has a Whisk Attachment: Remove the metal blade and install the whisk attachment. Add to the workbowl the egg white, the sweetening, and any additional ingredients called for in the recipe. Process 4 to 7 minutes, until the mixture becomes thick and fluffy and reaches the top of the whisk. Stop once to scrape the mixture from the side of the bowl. See Serving Suggestions.

If Your Food Processor Does Not Have a Whisk Attachment: Transfer the chopped fruit to a 2-quart or larger mixing bowl and add the egg white, the sweetening, and any additional ingredients called for in the Ingredient Listings. Beat with an electric mixer until the mixture becomes thick and fluffy and expands to four times or more its original volume. This may take from 4 to 8 minutes.

Serve immediately or place in an airtight container and store in your freezer. If your freezer maintains a temperature no higher than 5°F, you may freeze these desserts for several days. If the temperature in your freezer rises above 5°F, freezer storage for a few hours is fine, but after several days storage, ice crystals will develop.

Ingredient Listings

FROZEN BLUEBERRY FRAPPÉ

6 ounces fresh blueberries, washed and stems removed
If using dried egg whites, increase blueberries to 8 ounces.

Nutritional information per ½-cup serving:
  calories 60
  fat 0.1g
  saturated fat 0

(continued) ∿

FROZEN STRAWBERRY FRAPPÉ

~~~

6 ounces fresh strawberries (about 1⅛ cup), washed, hulled and cut in half if larger than 1 inch

If using dried egg whites, increase strawberries to 8 ounces (about 1½ cups).

FROZEN PEACH FRAPPÉ

~~~

8 ounces ripe peaches (2 medium), peeled, pitted, and cut into 1-inch pieces (about 1⅛ cup)

If using dried egg whites, increase peaches to 11 ounces (about 1½ cups).

1 teaspoon peach schnapps (optional)

Frozen Raspberry Frappé

~~~~~

9 ounces fresh raspberries (about 2 cups), washed and forced through a strainer or put through the power strainer attachment of a food processor or mixer to remove the seeds

This will yield about ¾-cup raspberry puree. If using dried egg whites, increase raspberries to 12 ounces (about 2⅔ cups), yielding about 1 cup puree.

Frozen Pear Frappé

~~~~~

9 ounces ripe pears (about 2 medium), peeled, cored, and cut into 1-inch cubes (about 1⅛ cups)

If using dried egg whites, increase pears to 12 ounces (about 1½ cups).

1½ teaspoons Williamine or other pear liqueur

Nutritional information per ½-cup serving:
calories 60
fat 0
saturated fat 0

Nutritional information per ½-cup serving:
calories 62
fat 0
saturated fat 0

FROZEN PINEAPPLE FRAPPÉ

~~~~

6 ounces peeled and cored fresh pineapple, cut into 1-inch pieces
(about 1⅛ cups)

If using dried egg whites, increase pineapple to 8 ounces.

FROZEN STRAWBERRY– BANANA FRAPPÉ

~~~~

4 ounces fresh strawberries (about ¾ cup), washed and hulled

2 ounces peeled banana (about ¼ cup mashed)

¼ cup sugar

If using dried egg whites, increase strawberries to 6 ounces and
sugar to ⅓ cup.

FROZEN BOMBES

~~~

It's easy to combine several of our frozen desserts in the colorful, make-ahead presentation that the French call a bombe.

For 6 servings, ⅔ cup each, use a 1-quart round bowl, or a 4-cup loaf pan or a 6-inch springform pan. Spread 2 cups of frappé, sorbet or frozen yogurt evenly over the sides to form a lining. Place in the freezer until firm, then fill the center with 2 cups of a contrasting color. Return to the freezer until firm. To unmold when ready to serve, invert the bowl or pan over the serving dish. Dip a towel into hot water, wring it out, and wrap it around the mold for a minute or two before lifting off the mold.

Strawberry or raspberry linings with peach or blueberry centers are attractive combinations. Bombes made with frappés are exceedingly light, while sorbets and frozen yogurts make more substantial desserts.

Just enough fresh ginger gives subtle flavor to this modestly rich homemade ice cream.

Yield: 12 servings

Nutritional information per 3½-ounce serving:
- calories 320
- fat 27g
- saturated fat 17g
- protein 1.7g
- carbohydrates 19g
- sodium 29mg
- cholesterol 99mg

GINGER ICE CREAM

2 pieces fresh peeled ginger, each about 1 by 1 by ½ inch
1 cup sugar
2 cups heavy cream
2 cups light cream
1½ teaspoons vanilla extract
½ teaspoon ground ginger
Pinch of salt (optional)

With the metal blade in the workbowl, process the fresh ginger and the sugar until the ginger is finely chopped, about 30 seconds, scraping the bowl once. Add the remaining ingredients and process until combined, about 10 seconds.

Pour the mixture into an ice-cream machine and follow the manufacturer's directions. Allow to ripen for 2 hours before serving.

Food Processor Method: Pour the mixture into a 9-inch square baking pan and freeze for 1 hour. With the metal blade in the workbowl, add the semifrozen mixture; process for 30 seconds. Return the mixture to the pan and freeze for another hour. Return to the workbowl and process for another 30 seconds. Transfer the mixture to a serving bowl; cover with plastic wrap and freeze for 2 hours to ripen the flavor.

Soufflé Glacé aux Framboises

(FROZEN RASPBERRY SOUFFLÉ)

~~~~

Almond Meringue Rounds (recipe follows)
Raspberry Soufflé Mixture (recipe follows)

Using an 8-cup soufflé dish as a guide, draw a circle on each of 2 sheets of parchment paper; place one sheet, drawn side down, on 2 cookie sheets. Spray the parchment paper with nonstick spray.

Prepare the soufflé dish: Fold a sheet of waxed paper about 2 inches longer than the circumference of the soufflé dish in half lengthwise. Spray the sheet with nonstick spray. Wrap the paper, sprayed side in, around the dish so it comes about 3 inches above the top of the dish; secure with tape.

Make the Almond Meringue Rounds.

Make the Raspberry Soufflé Mixture.

Assemble the Frozen Raspberry Soufflé: Spread about a 1-inch layer of the Raspberry Soufflé Mixture into the prepared soufflé dish. Top with an Almond Meringue Round. Add enough of the Raspberry Soufflé Mixture to have it come within 1 inch of the top of the dish. Top with the remaining Almond Meringue Rounds. Pour the remaining Raspberry Soufflé Mixture over the Almond Meringue Rounds and spread smoothly. Freeze for at least 4 hours. The soufflé may be frozen for up to 4 days. To do so, put it in the freezer until it is hard to the

(continued) ～

A *spectacular dessert from master-chef André Soltner joins rounds of baked almond meringue with layers of sweet and creamy raspberry soufflé.*
~~~~~~~

Yield: 20 servings

185
C o o l
O f f e r i n g s

*Nutritional information
per 3-ounce serving:*

calories 230

fat 11g

saturated fat 5.7g

protein 4.3g

carbohydrates 30g

sodium 45mg

cholesterol 33mg

touch. Then put a large plastic bag upside down over the soufflé dish and slip a large rubber band over the plastic bag to hold it tightly against the dish. If the soufflé has been frozen for more than 6 hours, remove from freezer and refrigerate about 60 minutes before serving. Before unwrapping, push the thin blade of a knife straight down into the soufflé halfway between the center and the edge. If the mixture feels too hard to slice for serving, let stand longer. Do not unwrap until ready to serve. At serving time, garnish the soufflé with fresh raspberries.

ALMOND MERINGUE ROUNDS

½ cup sugar

¾ cup blanched almonds

3 large egg whites [or 3 tablespoons dried egg whites and 4½
      tablespoons water (see page 39)]

¼ teaspoon cream of tartar

Preheat the oven to 250°F. Place 1 oven rack in the center of the oven and another rack in the next position below the center. (If the cookie sheets fit side by side, leave the rack in the center.)

With the metal blade in the workbowl, process ¼ cup of the sugar and the almonds until the almonds are finely ground, about 1½ to 2 minutes, scraping the bowl as necessary; reserve.

In a large mixing bowl, beat the egg whites [or the dried egg whites and water] with the cream of tartar until foamy; gradually beat in the remaining ¼ cup of sugar and continue beating, if necessary, until the whites are stiff. With a spatula, gently fold the reserved almond mixture into the egg white mixture to make an almond meringue.

Put the almond meringue into a pastry bag fitted with a ½-inch plain tube; pipe onto the prepared cookie sheet, starting at the center of each circle and piping in a spiral to the edge; the layers should be about ½ inch thick. Place both sheets in the preheated oven and bake until dry to the touch, about 1 hour. Remove with a wide spatula to a wire rack to cool completely; peel off the paper. The meringues should fit flat inside the 8-cup soufflé dish; trim to fit if necessary. Use as directed.

RASPBERRY SOUFFLÉ MIXTURE

⅔ cup water

2 cups sugar

10 large egg whites

2 twelve-ounce bags unsweetened frozen raspberries, thawed and refrigerated

2 cups heavy cream

2 teaspoons framboise

To a 2-quart saucepan add the water and the sugar; bring to the boil over medium-high heat. Boil until the syrup registers 260°F on a candy thermometer. In a large mixing bowl, beat the egg whites until foamy; gradually pour the syrup in a very thin stream into the egg whites, beating as you do so, and continue to beat until very thick. Cover and refrigerate; use as directed.

Drain the raspberries; force them through a fine mesh strainer or put them through the power strainer of a food processor or a mixer to remove the seeds. Stir the raspberry puree and the framboise into the beaten egg white mixture until there are no streaks. If the mixture is not cold, refrigerate it until it is.

In a medium bowl, beat the cream until stiff. Fold it into the cold raspberry and egg-white mixture, until there are no streaks. Use as directed.

Baked Alaska, once a prestige restaurant dessert, consists of ice cream mounded on a layer of cake, the whole covered with meringue and baked in a very hot oven just long enough to color the meringue and give it a hint of toasted flavor. Originally Baked Alaska was a challenge to the chef, but today, with the freezer and the microwave, it's an easy and delicious make-ahead.

~~~~~~~~~

Yield: 16 servings

188
C o o l
O f f e r i n g s

RASPBERRY ALMOND BAKED ALASKA
~~~~

1 quart vanilla ice cream
1 Pain de Gênes Base for Baked Alaska, page 32
2 teaspoons white raspberry brandy, such as framboise (optional)
1 tablespoon seedless raspberry preserves
4 large egg whites
½ teaspoon cream of tartar
1 cup sugar
1 teaspoon vanilla extract
½ teaspoon almond extract
½ cup sliced almonds (optional)

Line a 7-inch-wide 1-quart bowl with plastic wrap and fill it with the slightly softened vanilla ice cream. Cover with plastic wrap and use a rubber band to hold the wrap in place. Place the bowl in the freezer at least overnight or up to 3 days.

Prepare the Pain de Gênes Base for Baked Alaska. After it has cooled to room temperature, spray an inverted 9- or 10-inch springform pan bottom with nonstick spray and place the cake on it. Brush with the raspberry brandy and spread with the raspberry preserves. Remove the bowl of ice cream from the freezer and unmold it onto the reserved cake. There should be a ½-inch border all around. Reserve in the freezer.

Place a rack in the lower third of the oven and preheat to 500°F. Soak the sliced almonds in water, drain, and reserve.

In a 2-quart or larger bowl beat the egg whites and the cream of tartar until soft peaks form. Continue beating, gradually adding the sugar, until stiff peaks form. Beat in the vanilla and the almond extracts.

Remove the cake and ice cream from the freezer. With a flat spatula, spread the meringue evenly and smoothly over the entire surface of the ice cream and the side of the cake; the meringue layer must seal the cake completely and be at least ¾ inch thick everywhere, with no thin spots. Sprinkle the reserved almonds over the meringue. Place the cake on a baking sheet and bake only until lightly browned, 2½ to 3½ minutes. Check after 2 minutes.

Slide 2 wide flat metal spatulas between the pan bottom and the baking sheet and remove the dessert to a serving dish. Serve immediately, or freeze for up to 3 days. To serve after freezing, let stand only until soft enough for a cake tester or skewer to penetrate the ice cream without forcing. Or, with 2 dry paper towels under the pan bottom, microwave at medium-low setting, checking and turning every 15 seconds, until softened. Serve immediately.

Nutritional information per 3⅓-ounce serving, with original Pain de Gênes cake base and rich ice cream (16% butterfat):

calories 232

fat 12g

saturated fat 5.9g

protein 4.2g

carbohydrates 28g

sodium 45mg

cholesterol 53mg

Nutritional information per serving with modified Pain de Gênes cake base and regular ice cream (10% butterfat):

calories 206

fat 9.3g

saturated fat 2.9g

protein 4.2g

carbohydrates 28g

sodium 46mg

cholesterol 27mg

INDEX

∾∾∾